WordPress Website Owner's Manual 2018

The Illustrated User's Guide for WordPress Websites and Blogs
By Marsha Perry

Get free WordPress tips at http://www.perryweb.com

Disclaimer

The information provided within this book is for general informational purposes only. While the author attempts to keep the information up-to-date and correct, there are no representations or warranties, expressed or implied, about the completeness, accuracy, reliability, suitability or availability with respect to the information, products, services, or related graphics contained in this book for any purpose. Any use of this information is at your own risk.

The author does not assume and hereby disclaims any liability to any party for any loss, damage, or disruption caused by errors or omissions, whether such errors or omissions result from accident, negligence, or any other cause.

The information contained within this book is strictly for educational purposes. If you wish to apply ideas contained in this book, you are taking full responsibility for your actions.

Some links in this book are affiliate links. If you make a purchase through these links, the author will get some compensation. However, the author only recommends products that she would recommend to friends and family. Please do your own research and investigation before making any purchase.

Table of Contents

Introduction

Congratulations! You've got a WordPress website. Maybe you had a developer build it for you. Maybe a website host or friend got your site started. However it happened, you're the proud owner of a website powered by WordPress!

Now that some time has passed you'd like to make some text updates. You've heard about sites getting hacked and want to keep your site safe. Also, you'd like to show up in the search engines and get some business. Wasn't the point of getting a WordPress site that you'd be able to do some of these things yourself? At the moment it looks pretty complicated and you're not sure where to start.

The problem is that you're missing a key piece of the puzzle. Your site didn't come with an owner's manual. So here it is! In these pages I'll tell you what you need to know to manage, update and take care of your WordPress website. I'll keep it short and sweet.

My name is Marsha Perry, and I'm a website developer. I have WordPress websites of my own *and* I help small business owners with their WordPress sites. It's not an exaggeration to say that I work with WordPress every day.

You should know that I haven't always been a website developer. Ages ago, I worked as a bookkeeper. I mention this because I want you to know that I've been where you are right now. I've been overwhelmed by technical applications and wondered if I bit off more than I could chew. I got through it, and I'll get you through it too!

This is the second version of this manual. The first version was published in 2016. This version of the manual was written in January and February of 2018. It's been updated for WordPress 4.9.4 and has a current list of helpful plugins. In addition, I've learned a trick or two since I wrote the first version of the book.

So are you ready to start your coaching session? I promise to keep the technobabble to a minimum.

What's What?

Some of you might have WordPress websites and others might have WordPress blogs. No matter what you're doing with WordPress, this manual will help.

You should know that this book is written for people with self-hosted websites. That means you have a hosting account at a company like GoDaddy or SiteGround.

Some people host their site at WordPress.com. If that's the case with you, this book will still be valuable. However, I may touch on features or issues that aren't applicable to you.

Parts of Your Website

While everyone's website is different, there are some commonalities. Let's take a look at the various sections that make up a website. This will also help us to speak the same language later in the book.

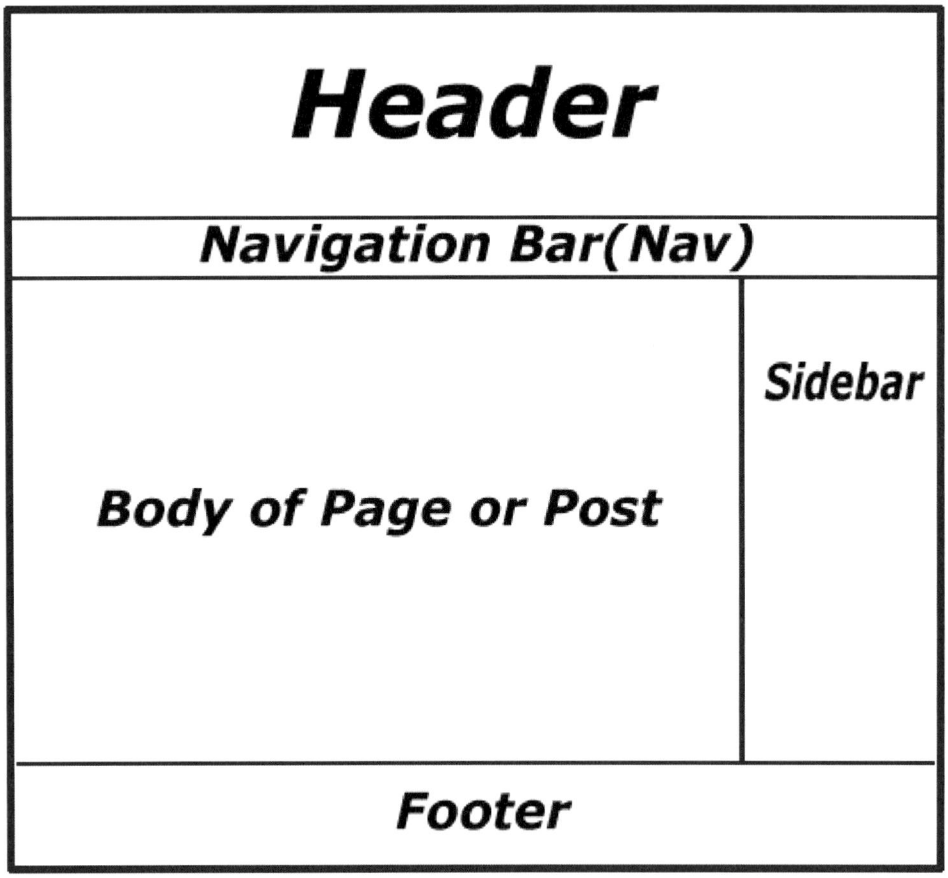

Header

Navigation Bar(Nav)

Sidebar

Body of Page or Post

Footer

The diagram shows the most common layout for a website. Yours might be a little different, but that's OK.

When I talk about the header, I mean the area at the top of your website. The footer is the area at the bottom of the site and the sidebar is on the side. Pretty easy, right? You'll find that many aspects of working with websites is quite straight forward.

The diagram shows one sidebar on the right. However, your website might not have a sidebar at all, or you might have two - one sidebar on the right and one sidebar on the left.

The navigation bar, that's the place with links to different pages of your site, typically runs along the top of the site. Some people have websites with vertical navigation areas in the sidebar.

WordPress Dashboard

When I talk about the WordPress dashboard, I am referring to what you see after you log into your WordPress software. Don't know how to log in to your dashboard? Go to YourSite.com/wp-login.php and enter your username and password. Then you'll see the dashboard. Here's the left side of a typical dashboard.

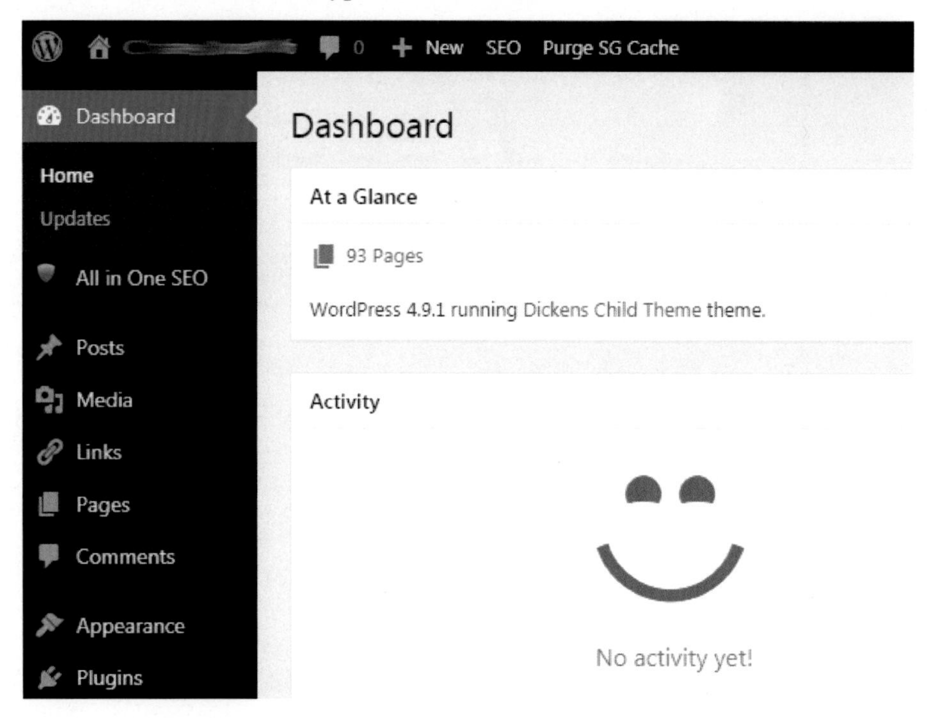

Difference Between Pages and Posts

WordPress sites are made up of pages and posts. While the main editing area for them looks the same, pages and posts are different.

WordPress Pages

- Are stand-alone items like service, privacy or contact pages
- Do not have categories or tags
- Usually have commenting turned off
- Can be "nested" or put into a hierarchy on a menu

It may be helpful to keep in mind the phrase ***website pages.***

While your screen may look a little different, here are the items that are commonly in the *right* column when you edit or add a WordPress Page:

- Publish
- Page Attributes
- Featured Image

WordPress Posts

- Can be put into categories
- Have tags
- Usually have commenting enabled

It may be helpful to keep in mind the phrase ***blog posts***.

While your screen may look a little different, here are the items that are commonly in the right column when you edit or add a WordPress post:

- Publish
- Format
- Categories
- Tags
- Featured Image

Quick Start Guide

Now that you've got a few basics down, let's move to some of the most common questions I get in my coaching sessions. Knowing how to do these basic tasks will probably take care of your most pressing needs when it comes to updating your website.

Updating or Adding Pages and Posts

"How do I edit and update my site's pages?" That's probably the most frequently asked question I hear during coaching sessions.

Don't worry. Text changes are easy to make.

Go to your site's dashboard. If you want to edit a post, click on *Posts*. If you want to edit a page, click on *Pages*. Hover over the title of the page or post you want to edit. You can either click on the title itself or click on *Edit* in the submenu that appears below the title.

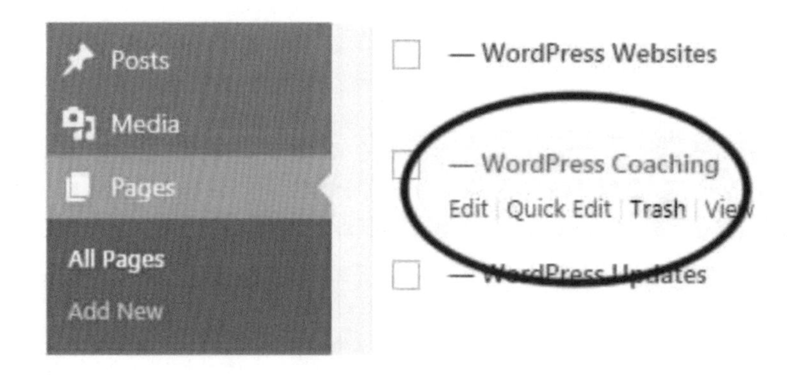

Next, you'll see the editing area. Make sure that you're looking at the editor in the visual view. The visual view has handy tools for you to use when editing your posts and pages. The text view gives you a view of the underlying HTML used in your page. (HTML is a coding system that makes up website pages.) While looking at the HTML can be useful sometimes, it can also be a little off-putting. You'll be happy to hear that you'll spend 99% of your time working with the user-friendly visual editor.

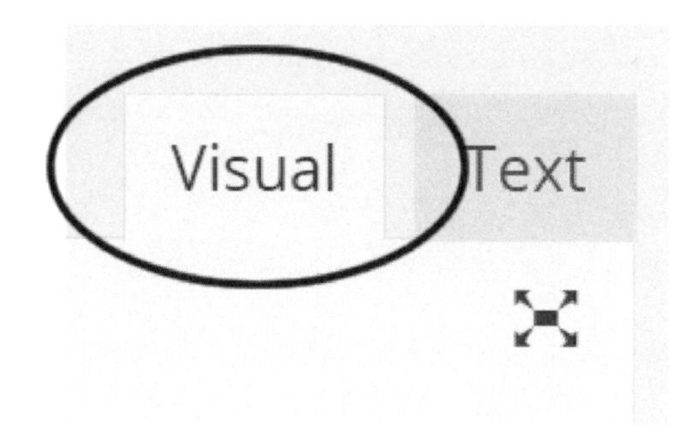

Right away you'll notice similarities between the editing tools in the visual view and other programs that you've probably used. I always compare the editing area to Microsoft Word or an email program. If you have questions about specific icons in the editing area, don't worry. I will cover every, single one of those icons later in the book.

Find the text you want to change and update it just as you would edit an email or update a Word document. On the right side of the page, in the *Publish* block, you'll see an *Update* button. Click on that to save your changes.

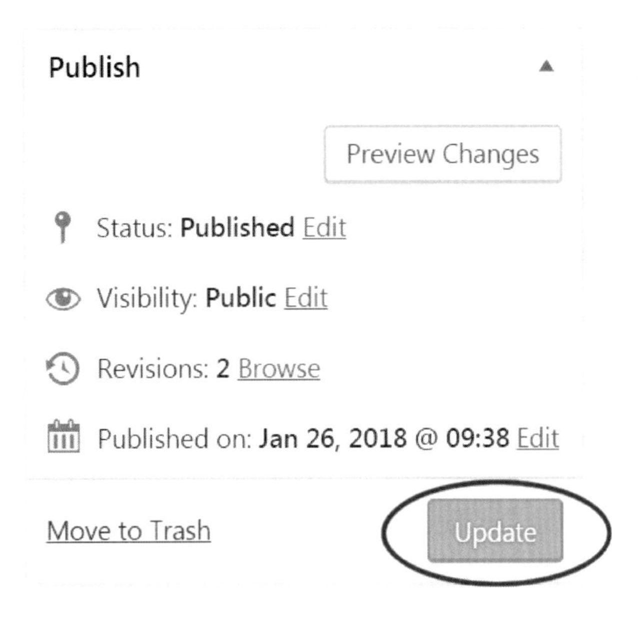

And that's it! You've made a text change in the body of your site.

What if, instead of updating a page or post, you want to add a new one? That's quite easy too. To add a post, click on *Posts* in the menu on the left and then *Add New*.

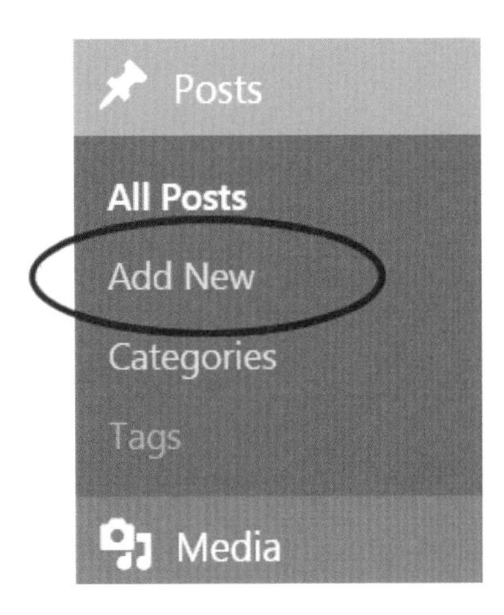

To add a page, click on *Pages* in the menu on the left and then *Add New*.

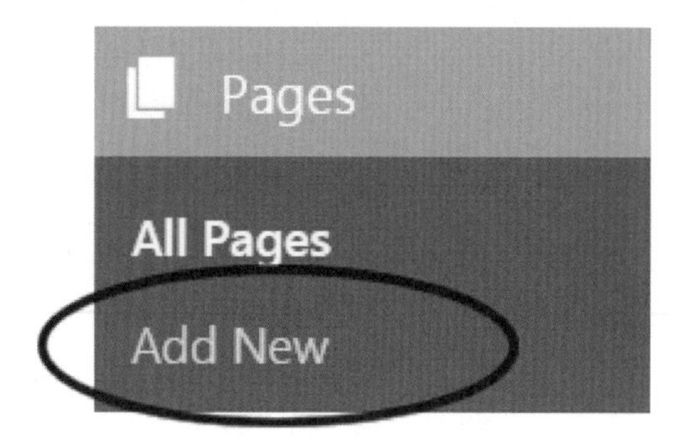

Add a title and some content. To save your work, click *Save Draft* in the Publish block on the right of your screen.

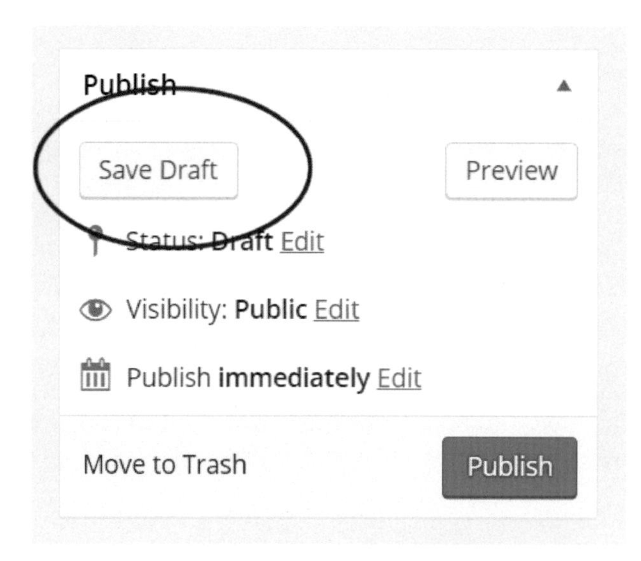

When you're ready to make your page or post live, click *Publish* in the Publish block on the right of the screen.

Once you've published a page or post **always** examine it in the public view of your site. By that, I mean, look at the new page or post as a visitor to your site would see it.

From within the WordPress dashboard you can click on *View Post* or *View Page* at the top of your screen. You can also open another browser window and navigate to your site. Once you're looking at your newly-published item, check the following things:

- Does the layout look as you intended?
- Is everything spelled correctly?
- Do all the links work?
- Do the photos look spot-on?
- Is the text accurate?

As someone who has worked on websites for years, I will tell you that it's important to go through the items on the list even if you're sure it's not needed. These checks are *always* needed.

So what if, despite your best efforts, you publish a blog post that contains a horrible, hideous mistake? That thing needs to be hidden from public view! Right now!

If you want to totally get rid of the page or post, select it as if you were going to edit it. Then click *Move to Trash* in the Publish block.

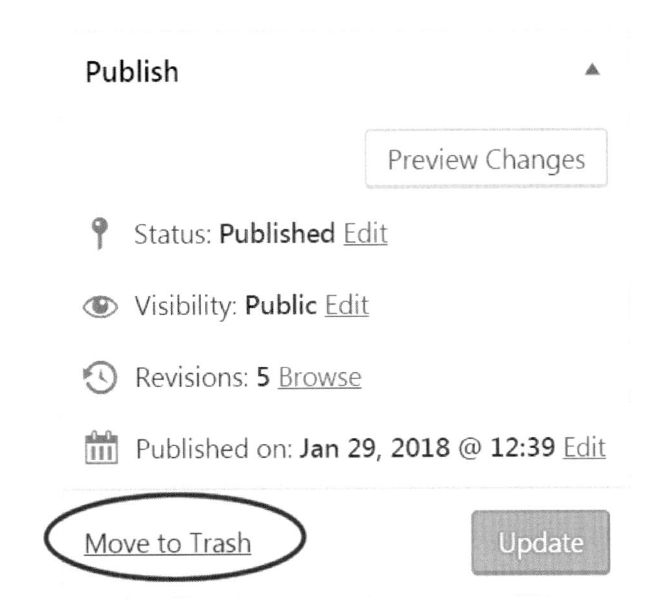

If you just want to get the page or post out of public view until it's fixed, you can turn it into a draft. Instead of putting it into the trash, click on the *Edit* button to the right of *Status: Published*. Then you'll see a dropdown box with various choices. Select *Draft* and then click *OK*. Then click *Update*.

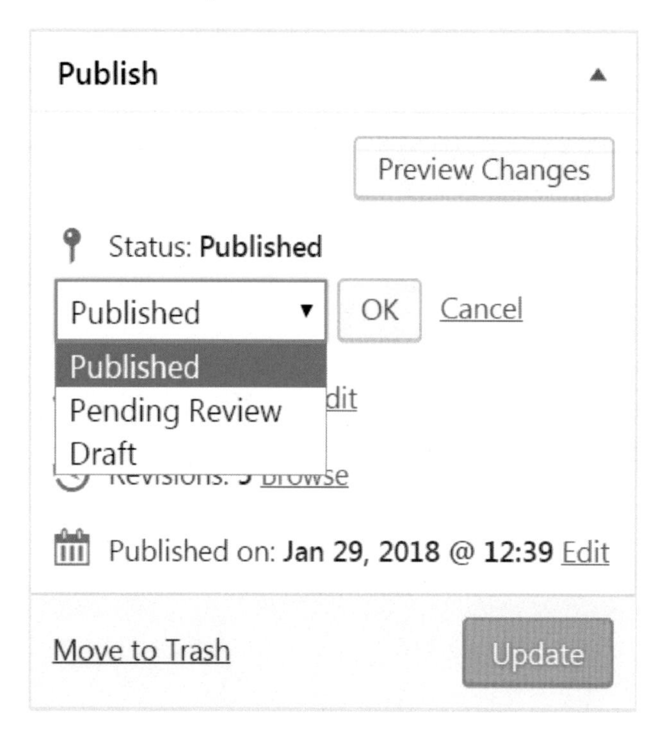

Your page or post is now a draft again.

Add Images

A picture paints a thousand words. You've heard that about a million times, right? The reason that it's such an enduring phrase is because it's true! Pictures illustrate points, draw people's interest and can be reused in social media.

To add a photo, go to the post or page that you want to edit. Place your cursor at the spot where you want your image to appear. Then click on the *Add Media* button at the top of the editor toolbar.

Then you'll see that you have two choices. If you want to reuse a photo already in the site, select *Media Library*. If you want to add a new photo, select *Upload Files*.

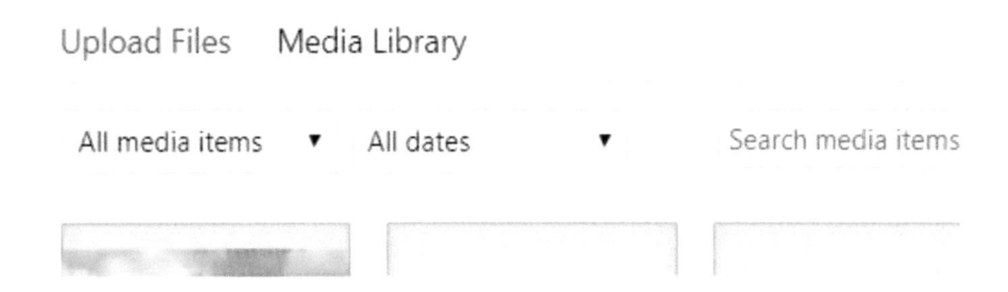

To upload a photo for the first time, select *Upload Files* and then *Select Files*. Now comes the tricky part. You need to remember where the image is on your computer. OK, I'm joking . . . I'm kind of joking. File systems can be tricky. At any rate, find the image you want to upload, click on it and select *Open*. Then you'll see the photo loading into WordPress.

Once the file is uploaded you'll see Attachment Details on the right of the screen. Use the slider bar to see all of the fields.

- **URL** – Don't make any changes here. This is the link to the image.
- **Title** – The system will automatically fill this in for you based on the file name. I like to replace it with a short term that describes the photo. This is also helpful for making your site perform well in search engines.
- **Caption** – Insert a caption here if you'd like one. Leave it blank if you don't.
- **Alt Text** – I use the same text that I used for the title in this spot.
- **Description** – I use this area for notes on where I obtained the image. However, you can leave it blank if you'd like.
- **Alignment** – A word of caution here, WordPress is not a system for tight, precise layouts. This isn't like working on a word processing program. Websites look different to people with different browsers, screen sizes and types of computers. You can align images, but I want to set expectations here. Simple layouts are best.

- **Link To** – You have tons of choices with this. Select *None* if you don't want the image to link to anything. Choose *Media File* if you want to link the image to the original version of the image. (This is handy if you add a thumbnail/small version of the image in the page or post. Then you can instruct people to click on the image to see a larger version.) You can select *Attachment Page*, but I've actually never seen a good reason to do this. You can also choose *Custom URL* to link to another page in your site or to link to a page in another website.

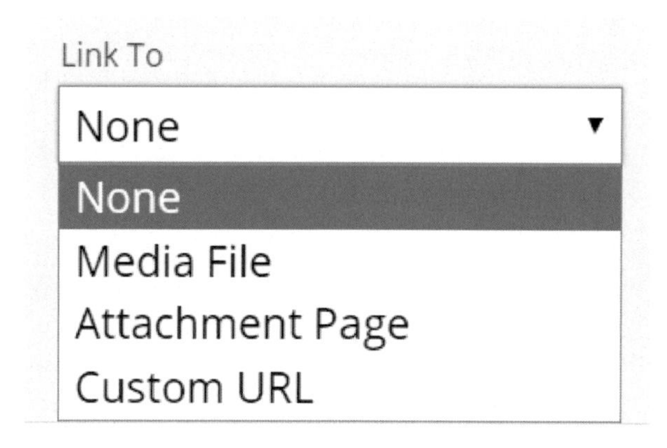

- **Size** – When images are loaded into WordPress, the software will make a few different versions of the image. The usual choices are full, medium and thumbnail. You can select which one you want to use. You can also select a custom size.

Adjust all the variables the way you want them, then click *Insert into post* and you've done it! You've added a photo!

To edit or delete a photo, click on the image and controls will appear above the image. You can change the alignment, edit the photo, or delete it.

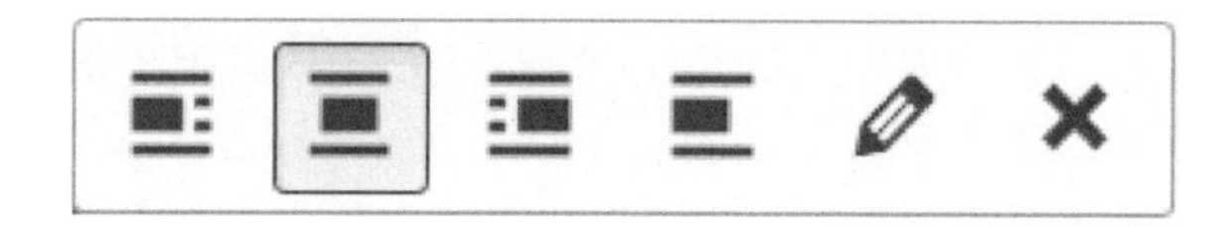

Add Links

Customers always ask me, "How do I add links?" So let's take a look at that.

From your page or post editor select the text that you want to link, then click the *Insert/Edit Link* control.

In this example I'm linking to the phrase "Click here".

Once you click on the link icon, a box will appear. That's where you enter the URL.

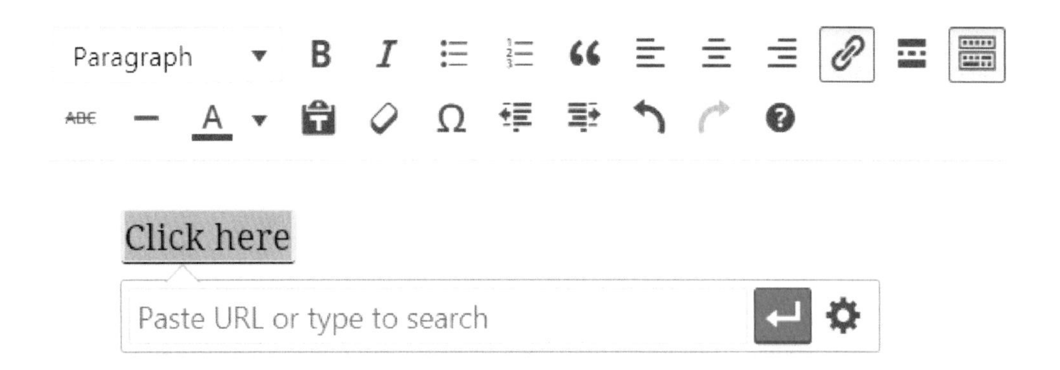

If you want to link to one of your own pages or posts, type some text in the box and WordPress will come up with a list of search results. Click on the one you want.

If you're linking to another website, be sure to start out the URL with HTTP or HTTPS.

Once the link is in place, click the blue icon with the arrow on it to insert the link. (That's the *Apply* icon.) For more choices, like the ability to open the link in a new tab, click on the icon that looks like a gear. (That's the *Link options* icon.)

To change or delete a link you've already added, select the linked text. A box will appear and you can either click on the pencil icon to edit the link or click the remove link icon to delete it. Note that you won't delete the text, just the link.

Working with Pages

Now that you're getting the hang of things let's take a look at the items to the right side of the WordPress editor. We'll look at pages first. As you'll recall, the items to the right of the page editor are:

- Publish
- Page Attributes
- Featured Image

We already talked about the *Publish* block. You use that to update or add pages.

Page Attributes

Next is the *Page Attributes* section. Note that you may or may not have the template attribute. If your theme has templates, then you'll have it. If your theme doesn't have templates (and that's totally okay) then you won't have the template attribute.

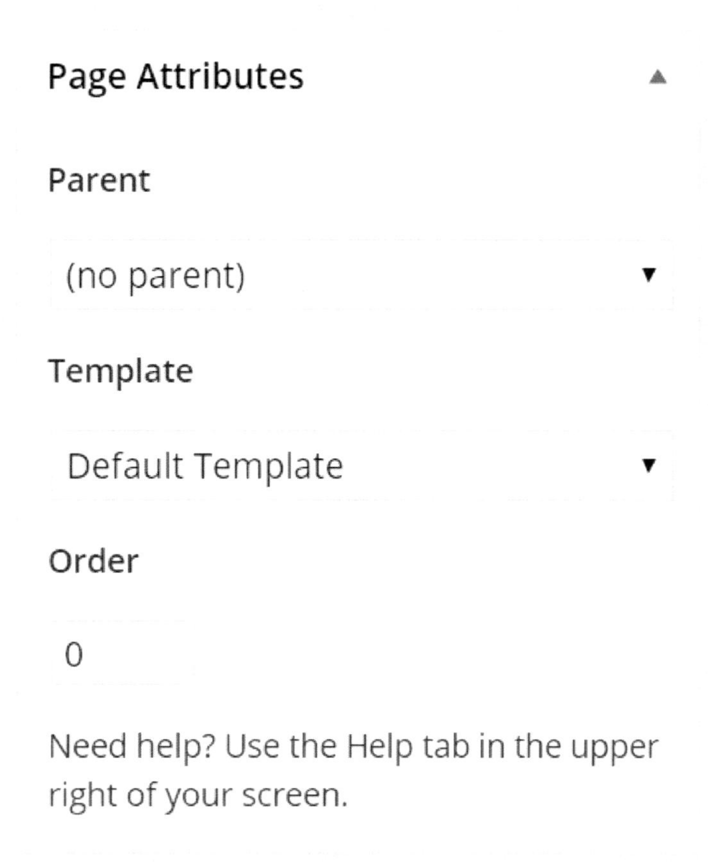

Parent Attribute - What in the world is a parent page? I'm glad you asked. The parent page feature allows you to create a hierarchy of pages. The page at the top of the structure is the parent. The *children* pages are below the parent. Often, but not always, this hierarchy will be echoed in your site's navigation. For example, here's the navigation for a website about Charles Dickens. The parent page is *Quotes*. The links below it go to the children pages.

Template Attribute - Some WordPress themes come with special page templates that allow you a choice of page layouts. If your theme offers templates, by all means experiment with them and see what each one does.

To see the templates click on the down arrow, select the one you want to use, and then save or update.

Here's an example of the templates available with one of my favorite themes, Weaver Xtreme.

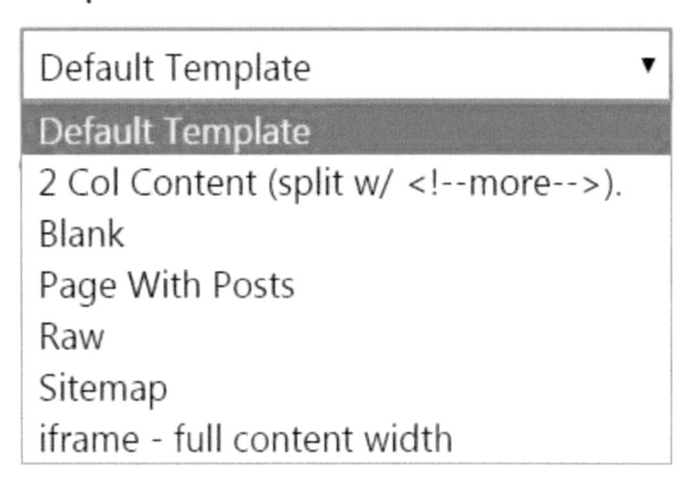

Order Attribute - Page order affects the site navigation. In most cases, pages will be displayed in the order that they are published.

What if you want the pages in a different order? There are a couple of ways to do that.

One way to change page order is to use the page order attribute. In a horizontal navigation bar the pages will be displayed with the lowest number on the left and the highest number of the right. Simply put a number into the order box and then save or update. When you're adding page numbers, it's best to order by tens (10, 20, 30, etc.) and leave some space between the page numbers. That way, if you add a new page later, you don't need to renumber everything.

Another way to update your navigation is to use custom menus. Check out the *Custom Menus* area of this book and then use the method which works best for you.

Featured Image

Next, I want you to look at the *Featured Image* block on the right column of your screen. Both pages and posts have featured images.

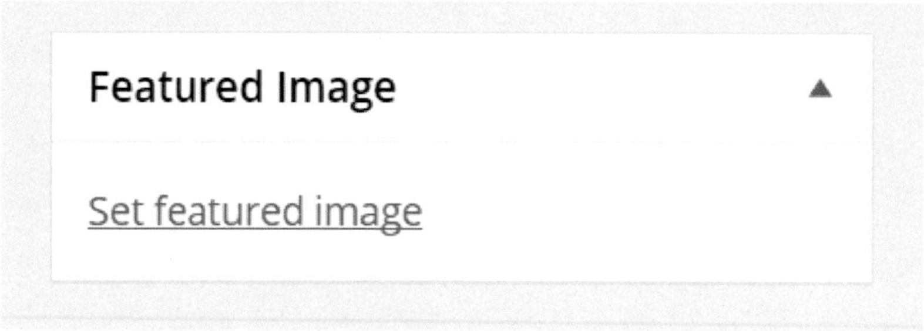

What the featured image does depends on your site's theme and plugins. Featured images may be used in slideshows, search results, the main blog page or the home page of your site. If you're sure that your site doesn't use the featured image then you can skip that section. If your site does use featured images click on *Set featured image* and you'll see the media library. You can add a new image, but usually people select an image already used in the page or post. Click on the image you'd like to use and then select *Set featured image*. Next you'd update or save.

After you've published a page or post with a featured image, be sure to view it as a visitor to your site would. With some themes, if the featured image is too big it will replace the header graphic. If that happens then you'll need to select a different graphic or upload a smaller image to use as the featured image.

That takes care of the blocks to the right of the page editor. Now let's looks at the post editor.

Working With Posts

As you'll recall, the blocks on the right of the post editor are:

- Publish
- Format
- Categories
- Tags
- Featured Image

Let's look at each of these.

Scheduling Posts in Advance

We've already talked about the *Publish* block, but now I want to show you a cool trick that you can use to schedule posts to publish in advance. In other words, if you want posts to appear while you're on vacation, you can set them up to publish before you leave. Do you want posts to go live early in the morning while you sleep in? WordPress will make them live while you snooze. This technique will work with pages too, but it's more commonly used with blog posts.

When you add a new post you'll see the Publish block on the right side of the page. Ordinarily you'd click *Publish* to make your post live.

Note the line above the Publish button that says *Publish immediately.* That's your ticket to being able to schedule content to publish at a later date!

Click *Edit* after *Publish immediately* and a scheduler appears. Select the date and time that you'd like your post to be published. Click *OK* and then *Publish.*

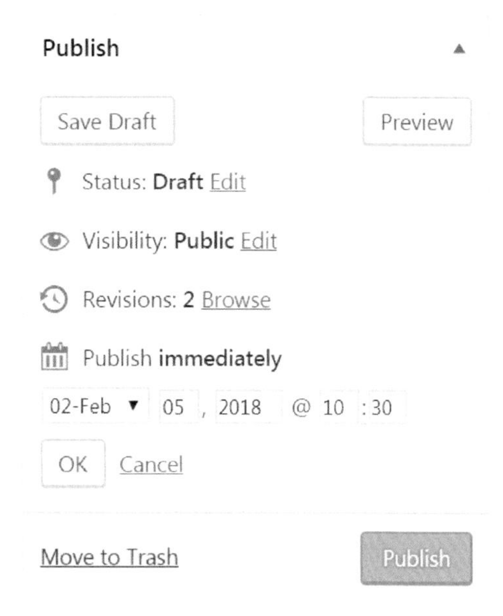

Your blog post is now scheduled, and will be published on the day and time that you specified.

Post Formats

This is the post equivalent of page templates. However, I've been blogging for years and *never* used post formats. Not even once. I just keep the setting at *standard.* Am I missing out? If you find a use for this feature let me know.

Post Categories

Blog categories are a way to help you group your blog post into subject areas. For a recipe site, categories may be something like *appetizers*, *breakfast* or *salads*.

Here are some of the most used categories on my blog:

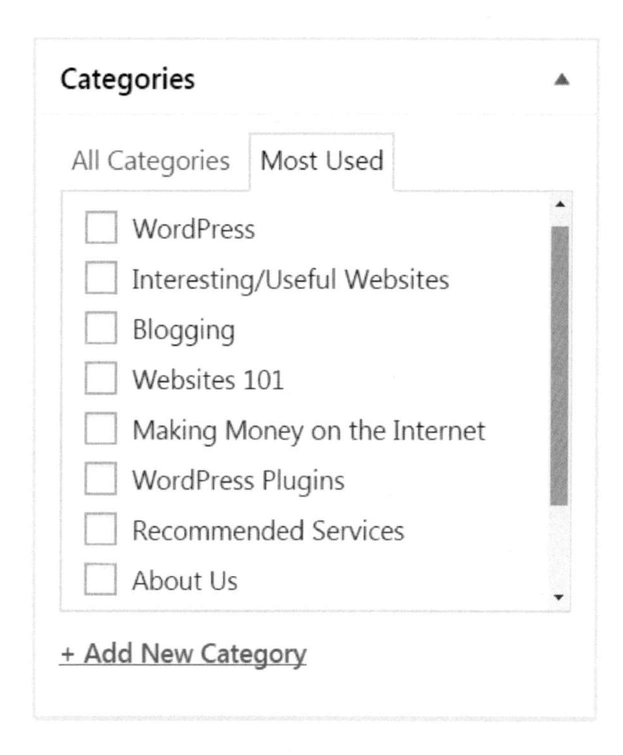

When you're thinking of category names, think of terms that people will type into search engines when looking for information on your site. Try to work those terms into the category names.

To add a post to a category, select the appropriate category, and then save or update the post.

To add a new category, click *Add New Category*.

Post Tags

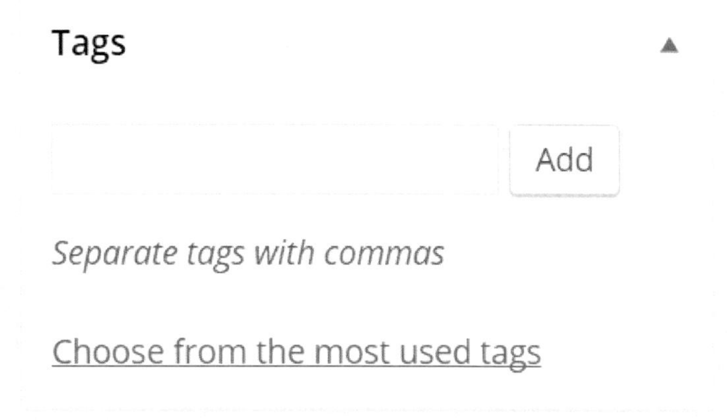

While categories describe your post in broad strokes, tags share specific details about the post's content. Let's say you're adding a recipe for Greek yogurt pancakes to a cooking blog. The category you use for this post might be something like *breakfast recipes* while the tags may be *Greek*, *pancakes*, *griddle* and *yogurt*. You can add as many tags to your post as you'd like. To add tags, simply type them into the tags field. Then click on *add*. Be sure to save or update your post.

You don't have to use tags. However, tags are sometimes used by search engines. Tags can also help visitors to your site find the information they seek.

Comments and Comment Spam

One feature that sets posts apart from pages is that visitors can usually leave comments on posts. The controls for comments are in the *Settings > Discussion* area of your dashboard. I recommend enabling comments, but always moderate them. That means that you'll approve comments before they're publicly viewable on your site.

Personally, I love getting comments from readers! First of all, it verifies the fact that people are reading what I write. Secondly, I get great ideas and feedback from comments.

However, there is a dark side to blog comments. It's called spam comments.

Spam comments are usually made by a computer program and contain links. The links go to places like pharmaceuticals companies, places to get loans fast or luxury watches. Sometimes the links are in the body of the comment and other times the links are in the URL of the "person" leaving the comment. Comment spam can be tricky because sometimes they try to look like real comments from readers.

These are all examples of spam comments I've received:

- "Nice post."
- "You have brought up a very great details, thanks for the post."
- "Some really nice and utilitarian info on this website, also I think the layout contains excellent features."
- "Your method of explaining everything in this post is in fact fastidious, all can effortlessly be aware of it, Thanks a lot."
- "I like this weblog so much, bookmarked."

A website owner can get *hundreds* of these a day. (I'm not joking!) So how do you keep from going crazy as you try to monitor the comments? You get a plugin that will help you. Antispam Bee or Cerber Security will get rid of most of the spam comments that come your way.

Toolbar Controls

We've already talked about some of the controls on the page/post editor. Here's a brief overview of *all* the controls of the editor and how they work.

Format Dropdown Box – Click on the triangle to see formatting choices for your text. The default mode is *paragraph*. The selection also includes various types of headings.

Bold – Highlight the text you want to bold and then click the bold control.

Italic – Highlight the text you want to italicize and then click the control.

Bulleted List – Put your cursor in the sentence or phrase that you want to be bulleted. Click the bulleted list control. To start your next item in the list just click the *enter* key. A new bullet will be created for your next item. Click the enter key twice and the system will know you're done with bulleted lists. It will remove any empty bullets and revert to normal type.

Numbered List – The numbered list control works just like the bulleted list control.

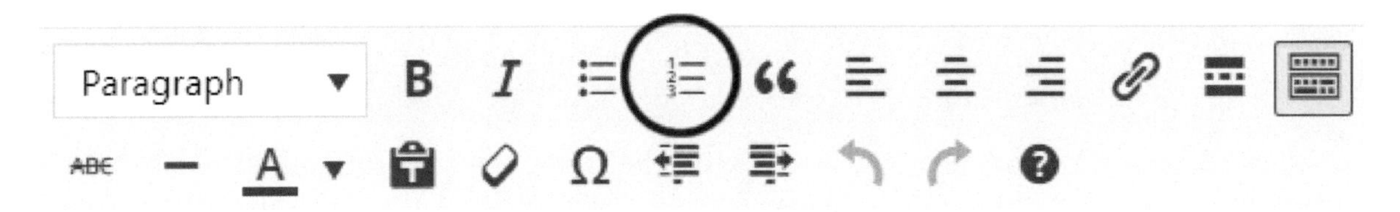

Blockquote – This control is used to emphasize a quotation from another source. Select the paragraph you want to feature and then click the control.

What will the blockquote actually look like? That depends on your theme. Some themes add a background color and a border. Some themes actually add quotation mark graphics. Be sure to experiment with your theme to find out what it does.

Left Align – Select the text that you want to be left aligned and click on the control. If you want to left align a whole paragraph, put your cursor anywhere inside the paragraph and then click the control. The whole paragraph will be left aligned. This applies to the center and right align tools too.

Center Align – Select the text that you want to be center aligned and click on the control.

Right Align – Select the text that you want to be right aligned and click on the control.

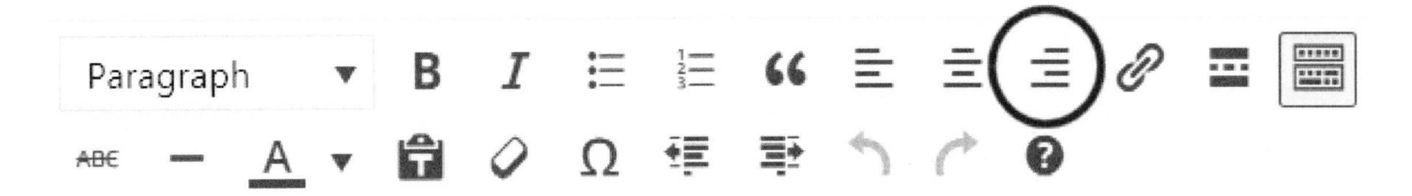

Insert/Edit Link - From your page or post editor select the text that you want to link or unlink, then click the insert/edit link control. See the quick start guide section of the book for detailed instructions on how to use this control.

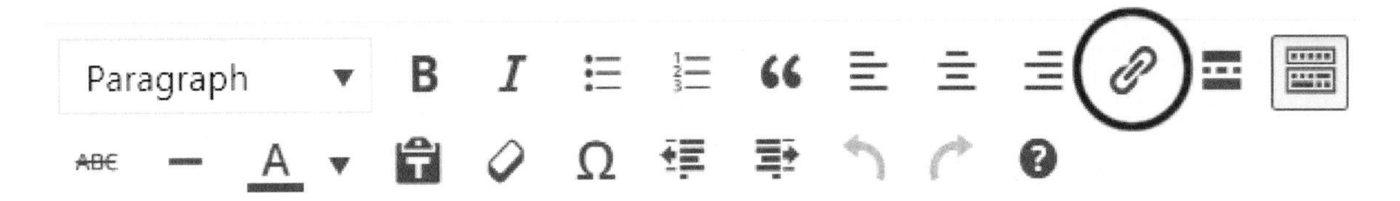

Insert Read More Tag – This button is used to create an excerpt for your blog posts. Excerpts can be used on the blog page, search results and on archive pages. Everything before the *read more* tag will be considered the excerpt.

However, I think there is a better way to make an excerpt. Look below the editing area of your blog post and you'll see the E*xcerpt* field. I find it easier to manually put text in that box instead of using the *read more* tag.

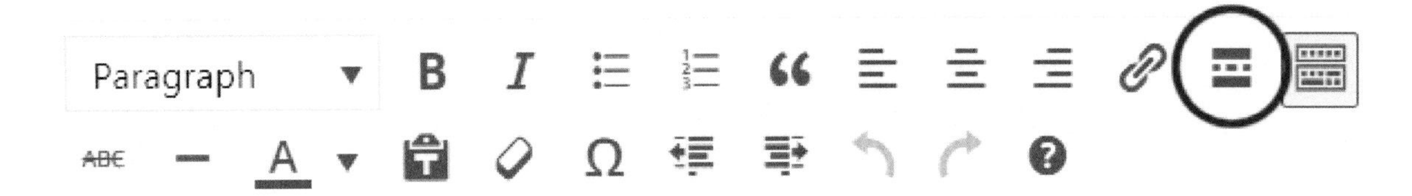

Toolbar Toggle – I am not a fan of this control. Sometimes I think its *only* purpose is to confuse new WordPress users. Click on the icon and you'll see what I mean. It hides the second row of icons on the editing dashboard. Click on it again to display the second row. I don't know how many times I've heard, "I know there are more controls, but I don't see them any longer." That's the toolbar toggle making trouble.

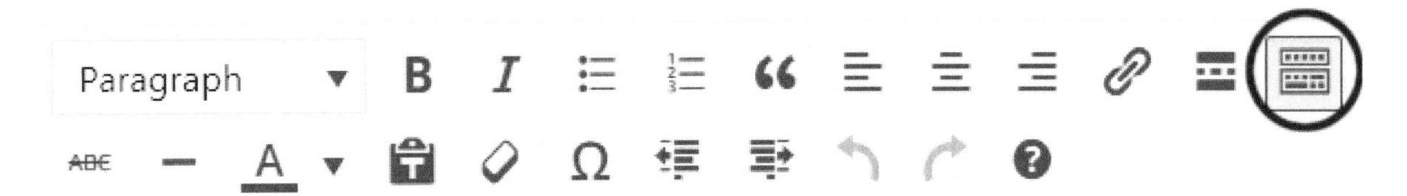

Strikethrough – Highlight the text you want to change and then click the strikethrough control.

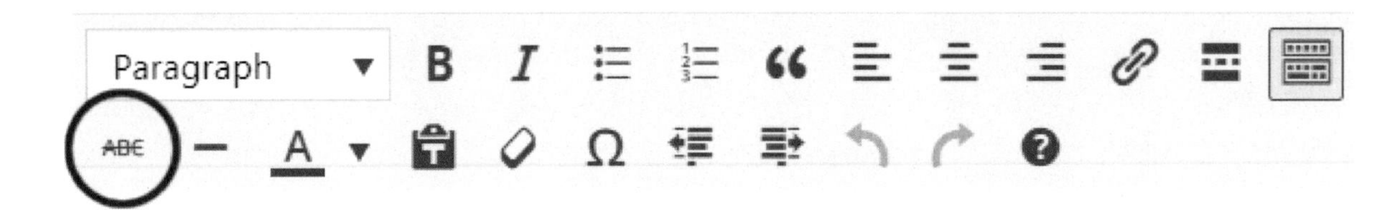

Horizontal Line – Click this button to add a horizontal line. Just to make sure that we're on the same page, this is *not* a dash. The horizontal line is a line across the page that usually acts as a divider between sections of text.

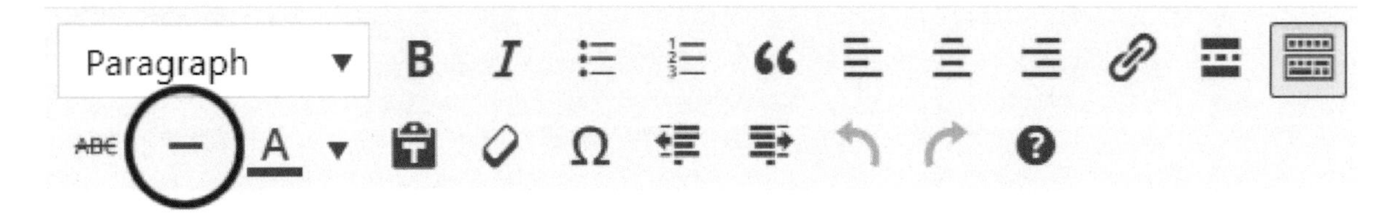

Text Color – Select the text that you want to color and then chose the color from this control.

Before you get too far along, let me give you my two cents on this control. I recommend that you use this tool sparingly. In fact, it might be nice if you *never* use it. When people first learn to use WordPress it's almost intoxicating. They have the power to make things appear on the web! If they want the text to be blue, then they make it blue. If they want text to be green, then they just go ahead and make it green. Suddenly their business website looks a little too colorful to be taken seriously. The lesson here is that just like eating a jumbo bag of M&Ms, just because you *can* do something doesn't mean that you *should* do it.

Paste as Text – If you copy and paste text into your editor, the bolding, links and basic formatting will be copied as well. (Things like fonts and colors won't be copied.) What if you don't want that? What if you want to copy *just* the text? Then click on this icon to remove links, bolding, and other basic formatting. Note that you must click on the icon again to get it back into default mode.

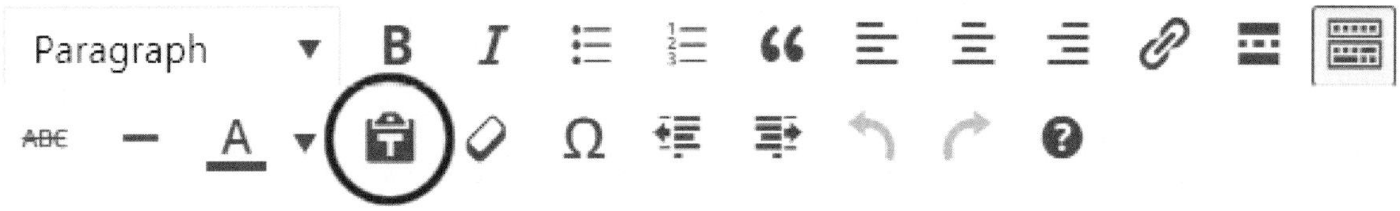

Clear Formatting – Use this tool to get rid of formatting. Just select the text you want to clear and click the icon. It will remove the styles, not links, from your text.

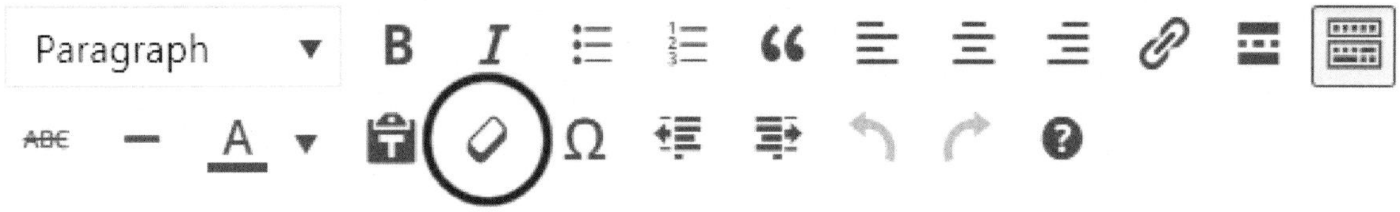

Special Character – Click on the special character icon and you'll see a large selection of symbols. Click on the one you want and it will be inserted into the editing area.

Special characters include the copyright symbol, the pound sign, letters with accents, and *tons* more.

Decrease Indent – To decrease the indent, put your cursor anywhere in the paragraph you want to reposition. Click on the icon. Presto chango! The text is moved!

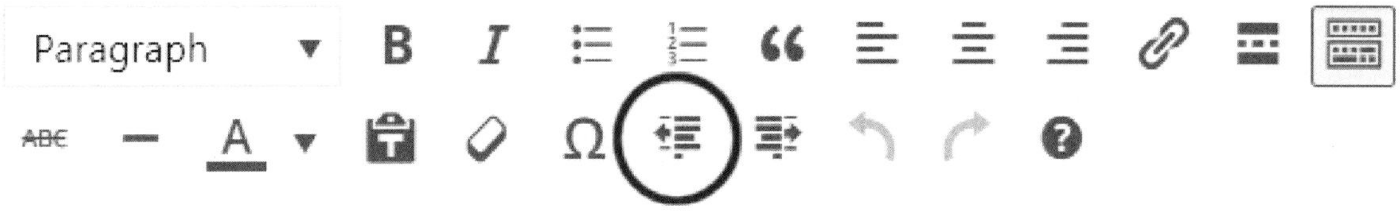

Increase Indent – This tool works the same way as the *decrease indent* tool. Put your cursor anywhere in paragraph that you want to reposition. Click on the icon and it's done.

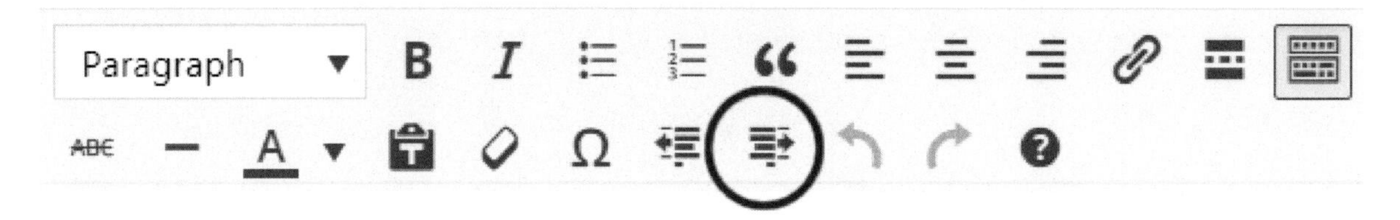

Undo – When this control is active you can click it to undo your last action.

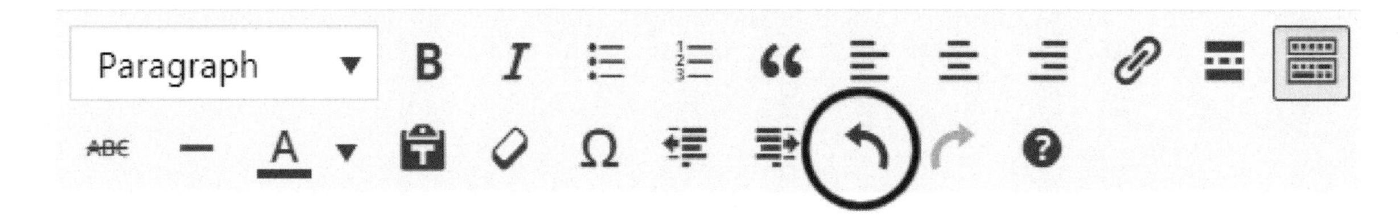

Redo – When this control is active you can click it to redo your last action.

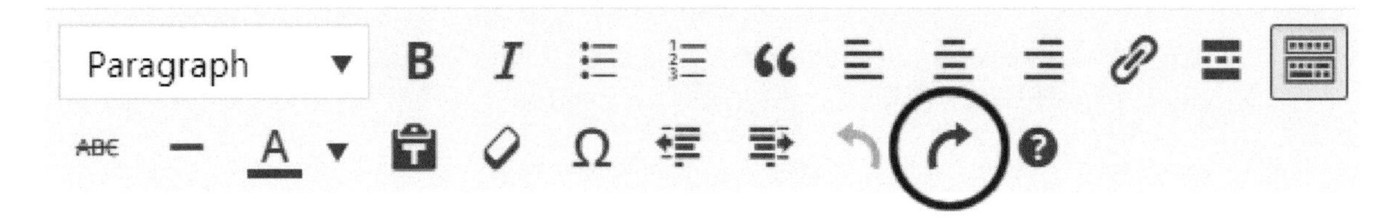

Keyboard Shortcuts – Click on the question mark icon to reveal a handy list of keyboard shortcuts.

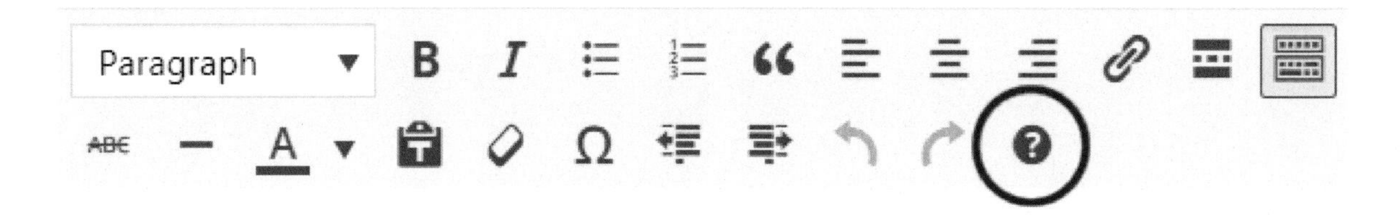

Plugins

WordPress plugins add functionality to your website. They're similar to cell phone apps, but for your site. For example: plugins can protect your site against hackers, make an email form, or help with search engine optimization. In February of 2018 the WordPress.org plugin directory contained 54,147 *free* plugins.

To see what plugins your site is currently using, go to your dashboard. Click on *Plugins > Installed Plugins*. Each plugin will have a short description. To learn more, click on *View Details* under the description.

Plugins may be installed in your system, but not turned on. Click on Inactive at the top of the page to see *just* the inactive plugins.

How to Delete and Add Plugins

Let's talk about deleting plugins first. It's insanely easy to do. Go to *Plugins.* Find the one you want to delete and deactivate it. Look at your site to see if anything broke. (If you're not sure, it's okay to leave the plugin deactivated for a time.) If your site looks fine, go back to the plugins area and click *Delete*.

You'll add plugins directly from your WordPress dashboard. That part is easy. Often the hardest part of adding a plugin is finding a suitable one. I like to start researching plugin at WordPress.org. (Note that there is also a WordPress.com website. That's not the site you want. Look for WordPress.org.) Once you're at the website, click on *Plugins*.

Type the name of a plugin you'd like to investigate, such as "Sucuri", into the search box. (Sucuri is a great security plugin that I'll tell you more about later.) You can also type in a word or phrase like "security".

Either way you'll see a list of possible plugins. This simple box gives you a lot of valuable information.

What sort of rating do people give the plugin? How many people have rated it?

Take a look at the active installations. I don't know about you, but I don't like being anyone's beta tester. I start getting interested in a plugin at about 750 active installs.

Once you find a plugin that looks interesting, click on its name or image to get more details. The plugin's WordPress.org page lists the last updated date. Look for a plugin that's been updated within the last year. Numerous problems can occur with plugins that aren't actively maintained. There could be security problems. There might even be compatibility issues with WordPress software.

Take a look at the features. Also pay attention to how the description is written. Is it full of technical jargon or is it written in a user-friendly way?

Be sure to look at the support forum. What sort of problems do people have with the plugin? Is the author responding to the forum?

Once you've found a plugin you like, go back to your WordPress dashboard. Click on *Plugins > Add New*. Type the name of the plugin you want to install into the search box. You'll see the same sort of results box that you did on WordPress.org. However, you'll also see *Install Now* in the top, right corner of each box. Find the plugin that you want and click *Install Now.* The plugin will be downloaded from WordPress.org. Turn the plugin on by clicking on *Activate*. How easy is that?

Once you've installed a plugin, the next step is to find its settings. The settings can be in a number of different locations. The first thing to try is to click Plugins and see if there's a settings link under the plugin's name. Here's how WP Cerber, a great security plugin that I'll talk more about later, looks after it's installed. Click *Main settings* and you'll go to the WP Cerber control panel.

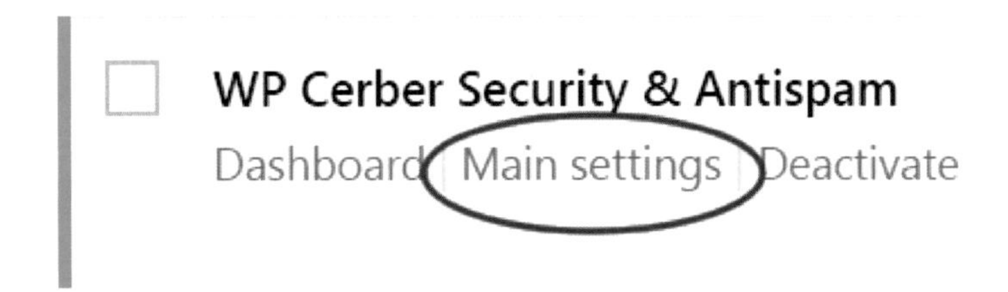

If you don't see a link to the plugin's settings under its name, look on the left side of the dashboard for anything new. If the plugin settings aren't there then look under *Settings*, *Tools* or *Plugins* sections on the WordPress dashboard.

Shortcodes

Sometimes the plugin instructions will say something like, "To add this to your site, copy and paste the shortcode into your website page or text widget." What?

Shortcodes are bits of computer code encased in square brackets. For example, if you use the Caldera Forms plugin you add contact forms to a page by putting code like this, [caldera_form id="CF5a7f66b9874ty"], into your contact page. There's no need to switch to the text editor, put the shortcode into the page using the visual editor. It'll be fine.

In other cases you might add functionality to your site by putting a shortcode in the sidebar. I'll go into this in more detail in the sidebar section of the book, but basically you add a text widget to the sidebar and paste the shortcode into the text widget. It's extremely easy.

Recommended Plugins

Here are some of my favorite plugins, organized by subject:

Form Builder:

Want to add a contact form to your site? Caldera Forms is well-documented and has tons of features. It can:

- send you an email with the form submission
- back up form submissions in case there's a problem with the emails
- send auto-responder emails to the person who filled out the form
- redirect visitors to another page after the form is submitted
- fight spam without the use of a CAPTCHA

Mobile Friendliness:

May I be honest? If your WordPress site isn't mobile friendly, you need a new theme. I've seen reports stating that about half of Internet traffic is from mobile devices. My own websites validate that number.

However, I also understand the realities of time and budget. A short-term fix for a theme that doesn't display well on mobiles is the WPtouch plugin. Be sure use the preview to see how your site looks. You can customize the colors and insert your social media links. For some sites the WordPress login will be displayed in the mobile menu. If this happens to you and you'd like to turn it off, go to *WPTouch > Settings > Menu Settings*. Look for the *Menu Options* section of that page. Turn the *Show login in menu* setting to the off (or red) position.

Page/Post Editing Tools:

- Advanced Image Styles – This plugin allows you to add borders and padding around images.
- Page Builder by SiteOrigin - Are you looking for a more complicated page layout? Page Builder can help you add columns or more advanced layouts. Once you've installed it, you don't have to use it on all the pages of your site. Just use it on the pages that you want.
- Tabby Responsive Tabs - I love this plugin! It's easy to use and makes cute, tabbed content that looks good on desktops, laptops and mobile screens.

Related Posts:

- Related Posts for WordPress – Who doesn't want more page views? This is handy to put at the end of posts to show visitors related content.

Search Engine Optimization (SEO):

- All in One SEO Pack handles Search Engine Optimization (SEO) for WordPress sites. It's flexible enough for the SEO novice as well as the SEO expert. It comes with a built-in sitemap maker that will send your site's information to Google and Bing.
- Simple 301 Redirects helps your SEO and gives visitors a better experience by sending them from an old or retired URL to the new location. I use this for site reorganizations and in cases where I've retired website pages or posts.
- Yoast is probably the most popular SEO plugin around. I don't use it, but more than 5 million other people do so it's worth a mention.

Shopping Cart and eCommerce:

- WooCommerce – I don't cover shopping carts in the book, but in case you're wondering WooCommerce is the shopping cart plugin that I recommend. It's well-supported, easy to use and runs like a champ.

Sidebar Widgets:

- Feature a Page allows you to easily highlight a page or post in a sidebar widget. Depending on your WordPress theme, you may be able to use it in the body of your pages and posts too. It uses the featured image and excerpt to make configuring the widget fast and easy. It doesn't hurt that it comes with three different built-in styles either.

Site Navigation:

- Search Exclude will hide pages, such as thank you pages, from your site's navigation and search.

Slideshows:

- Slider by Soliloquy makes it easy to add image slideshows.
- I've used Smooth Slider to create featured content slideshows on my own sites.

Social Media:

- Share Buttons by AddToAny – This plugin allows visitors to share your posts on Facebook, Twitter, Pinterest, LinkedIn and other social media sites.

Spam Fighters:

- Antispam Bee fights comment spam. It's easy to install and set up.
- Cerber, a plugin that's also mentioned in the security section, fights spam. You can even use it to add Google reCAPTCHA to your registration, contact and comment forms.

SSL (HTTPS)

Sorry to use jargon! If you want your site to be secure (if you want it to be HTTPS instead of HTTP) your site may need a little help. When you add a SSL certificate you *want* to avoid mixed content messages and you *don't* want to recode all your internal links. Really Simple SSL helps with those issues.

Maintenance:

- Optimize Database after Deleting Revisions provides website owners with an easy way to slim down the size of the WordPress database. That in turn helps make your site run faster.
- Maintenance Mode – Use this to display a message like, "We're sorry, but our site is currently undergoing scheduled maintenance. Please try back later." This is useful to have before the site is officially launched or when the site is having serious issues.

Website Backups and Security:

Because website security is *such* an important area, I cover the use of all of these plugins in the website security portion of the book.

- Cerber Security guards against brute force attacks by limiting the number of times someone can try to guess the WordPress dashboard logins. It also has some nice features like whitelisting your IP address and blocking IPs that try to get into the dashboard with nonexistent user names.
- File Manager – This tool helps you view and back up your website files.
- Sucuri Security does malware scans and hardens WordPress installations against hackers.
- WP-DB-Backup backs up your WordPress database.

Custom Menus

As we've discussed, often the default layout for pages in the navigation bar is to display the pages in the order they were published. You can override that by using *Order* in the *Page Attributes* area. However, there's a second method that you can use to control how your navigation is displayed. You can make a custom menu.

To access the custom menu section of WordPress, log into your dashboard and select: *Appearance > Menus*. Once you're there, you can either edit an existing menu or create a new one.

To make a new menu, click on *create a new menu* and then follow the instructions by giving your new menu a name. Then you can add pages, posts, custom links (specific URLs), categories, tags, or formats.

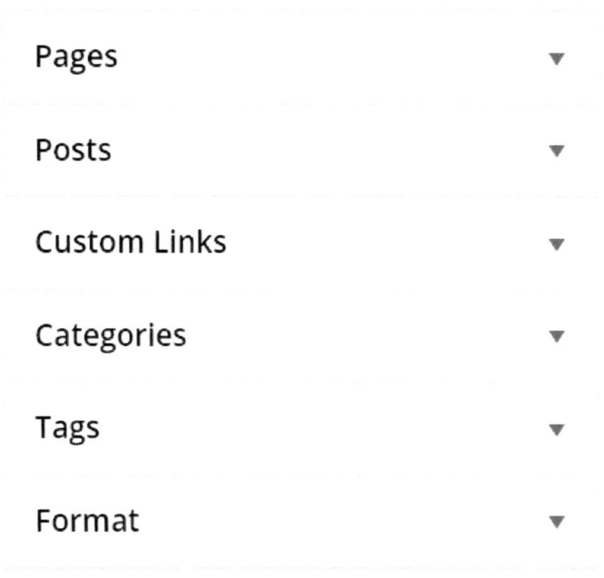

Pages ▼

Posts ▼

Custom Links ▼

Categories ▼

Tags ▼

Format ▼

If you don't see all of these choices click on *Screen Options* at the top right of the screen. Then you'll see more choices for your custom menus.

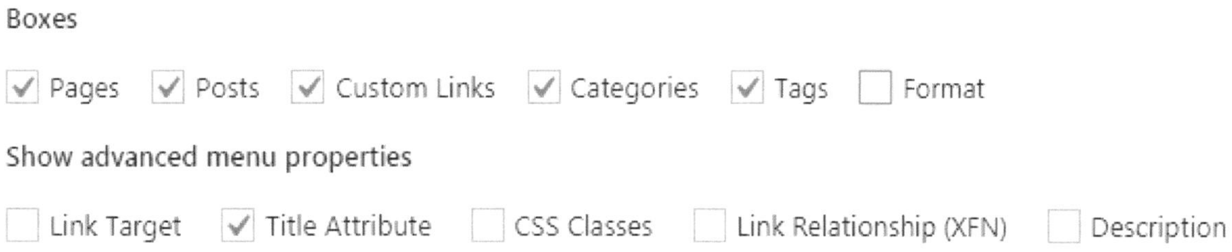

Boxes

☑ Pages ☑ Posts ☑ Custom Links ☑ Categories ☑ Tags ☐ Format

Show advanced menu properties

☐ Link Target ☑ Title Attribute ☐ CSS Classes ☐ Link Relationship (XFN) ☐ Description

Adding items to the menu is fairly straight forward. For example, here's a category list from a bread making site. Just select the categories you want to put in the menu, then click *Add to Menu.*

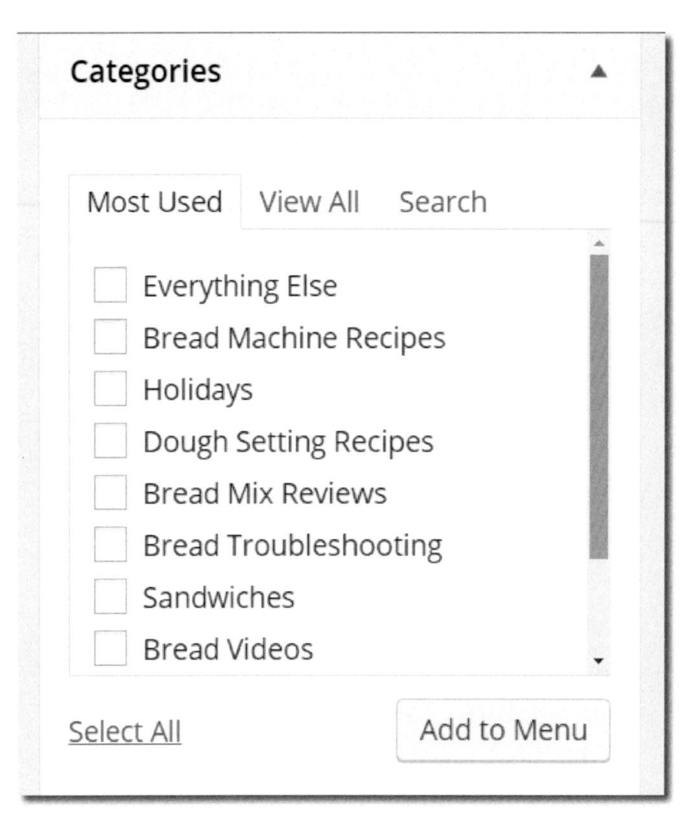

To add a link to another website use the *Custom Links* section. Put in the URL you want to link to, add the link text and then click *Add to Menu.*

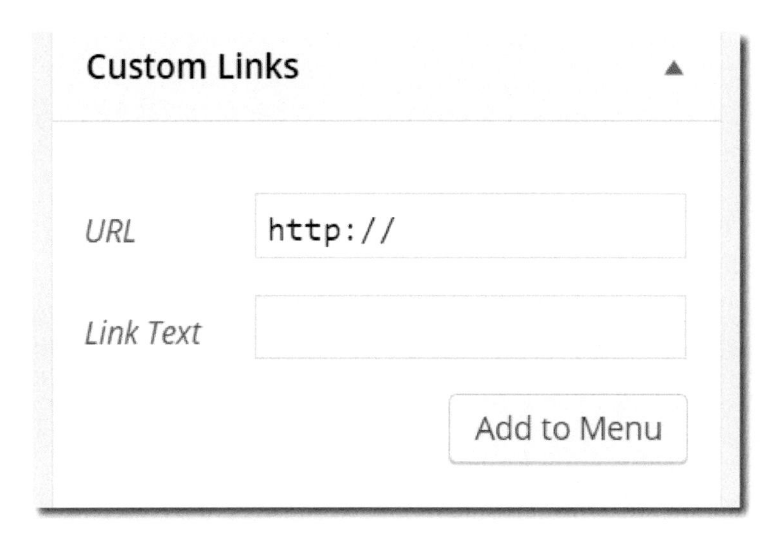

You can move menu items around so they're in the order you want. Just drag and drop them into place. You can have sub items too.

If you click on the arrow at the left of the menu item you'll see even more choices. You can have the menu text say anything you want. Just enter it into the *Navigation Label* area. Here's part of a custom menu from a website on Charles Dickens.

Quotes Page ▲

Navigation Label

Quotes

Title Attribute

Move *Up one* *Down one* *Under Life* *To the top*

Original: Quotes

Remove | Cancel

Daily Dose of Dickens *sub item* Page ▼

Random Charles Dickens Quote *sub item* Page ▼

Once you're done, be sure to click on the *Save Menu* at the bottom of the page. I don't know how many times I've forgotten to do that and wondered why the custom menu wasn't working correctly.

Once your custom menu is completed, how do you display it? There are two ways.

The first way is to use any menu locations that come with your theme. How the heck do you find that out? It's a lot easier than you'd think. When you're editing the menu you'll see the *Menu Settings* area under your menu structure. This shows where your theme accepts custom menus.

Here are the locations that come with the Weaver Xtreme theme.

Menu Settings

Auto add pages ☐ Automatically add new top-level pages to this menu

Display location ☐ Primary Navigation: if specified, used instead of Default menu

☐ Secondary Navigation: if specified, adds 2nd menu bar

☐ Header Mini Menu: if specified, adds horizontal mini-menu to header

If those locations don't work for you, or if your theme doesn't use custom menus, there's a second way to display the menus on your site. You can add custom menus to your site's sidebar. Go to *Appearance > Widgets* on your dashboard. Drag the *Navigation Menu* widget into the sidebar where you want to display the menu. (Don't worry if this sounds difficult. There's more information about widgets and sidebars later in the book. You'll find that working with widgets isn't bad at all.) Once the widget is in place you can add a title if you want. If you don't want a title, then leave that spot blank. Use the dropdown box to select the menu you'd like to add.

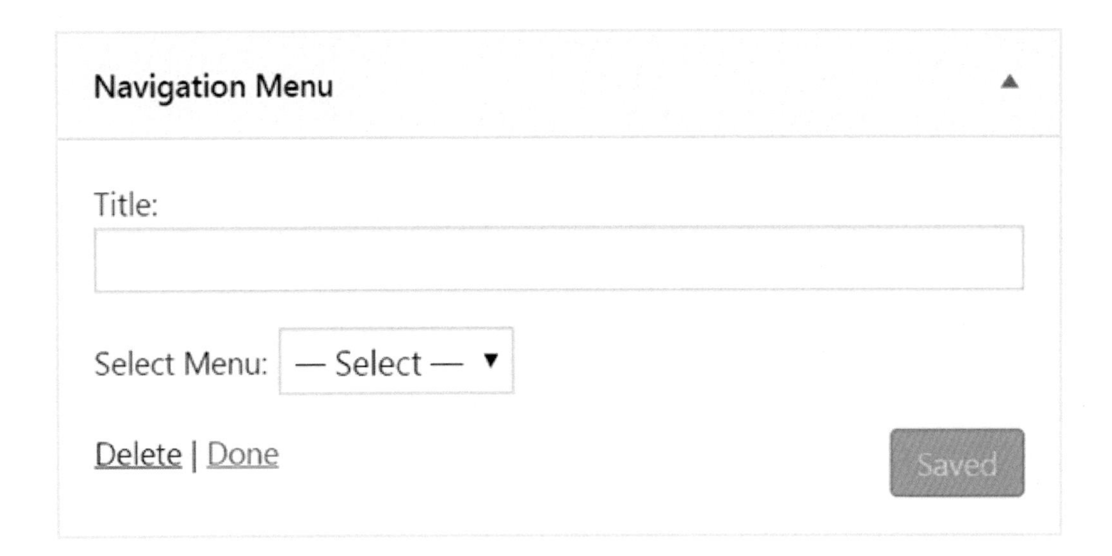

Working with Sidebars

Working with sidebars can be a little intense, but we'll take it one step at a time.

The first thing you should know about sidebars is that they're make up of blocks called widgets. This is a key concept, so let me say it again. Sidebars are basically containers for widgets.

Your sidebar might contain a widget for a newsletter signup and another widget with links to your social media accounts. Widgets can show popular posts, hold custom menus, display customer testimonials or be used to display affiliate ads.

There's no "sidebars" control on the dashboard. If you want to work with the sidebars you go to *Appearance > Widgets*. On the left of that page you'll see the available widgets. Here's how that looks in one of my websites.

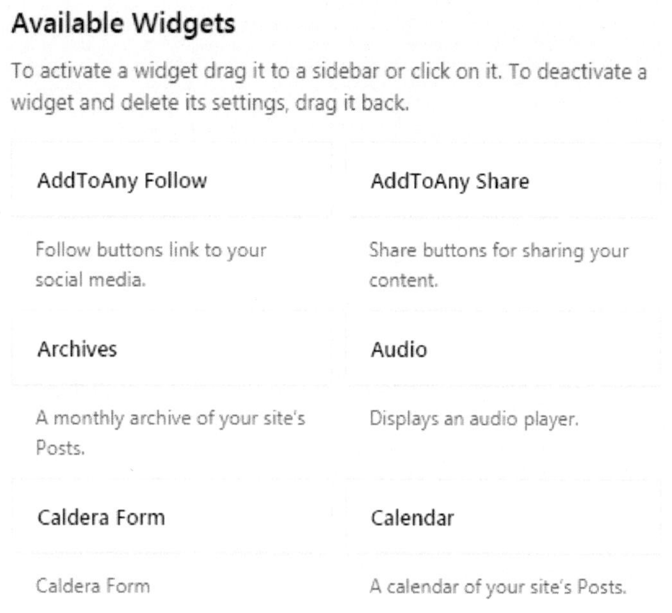

Available Widgets

To activate a widget drag it to a sidebar or click on it. To deactivate a widget and delete its settings, drag it back.

AddToAny Follow

Follow buttons link to your social media.

AddToAny Share

Share buttons for sharing your content.

Archives

A monthly archive of your site's Posts.

Audio

Displays an audio player.

Caldera Form

Caldera Form

Calendar

A calendar of your site's Posts.

The right side of the page holds the sidebar areas. That brings us to the second big thing about sidebars. Some themes have a *bunch* of sidebars, including sidebars for the header and footer. There may be different sidebars for pages and posts.

As an example, here are the sidebars for a site built with the Weaver Xtreme theme.

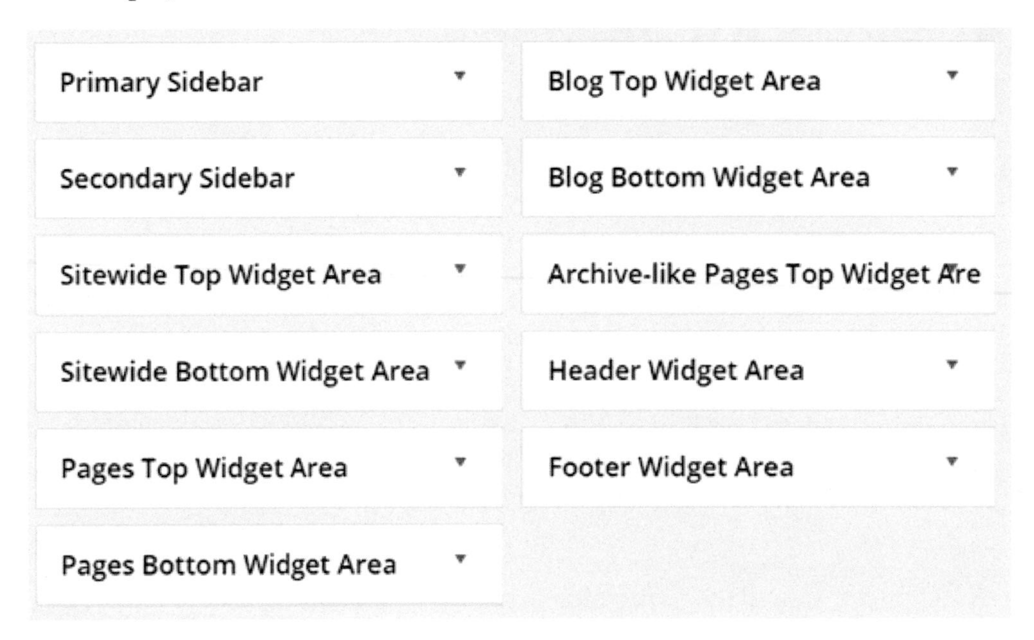

Each sidebar corresponds to an area on your site.

Note the arrow on each sidebar block. Click on that to expand the sidebar and see what widgets are being used. Here are the widgets used in the Secondary Sidebar of one of my sites.

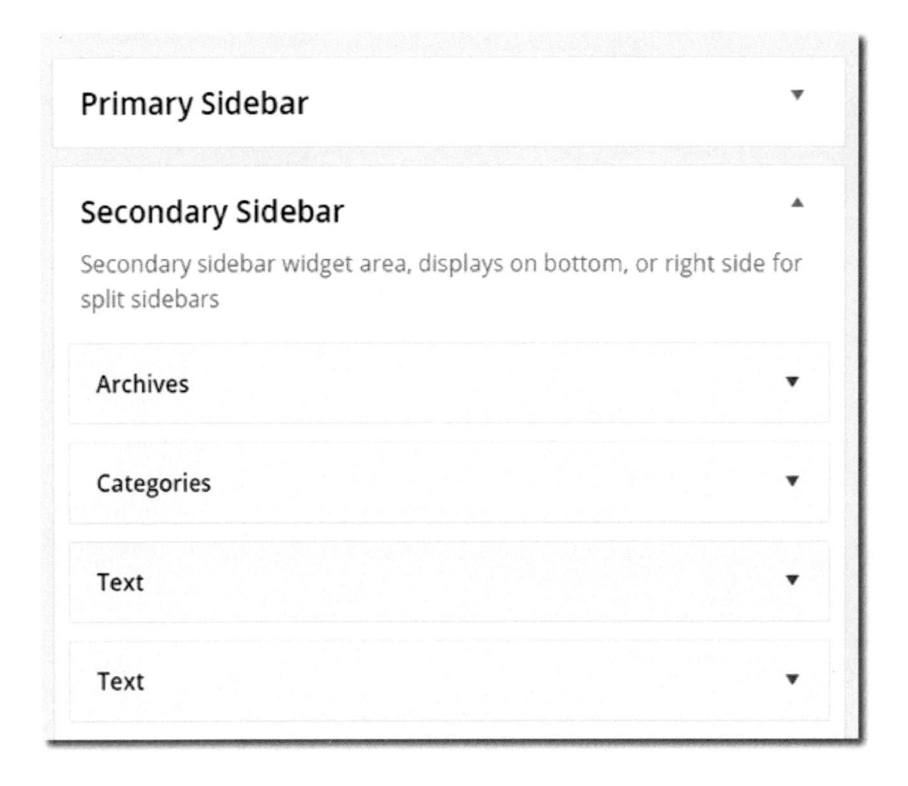

If you're having problems telling what sidebar goes where, open them up and see what widgets are inside each one.

If that doesn't help, put the site into maintenance mode using the Maintenance Mode plugin. Then use a text widget (I'll explain that in a second) with some tricky text like "Test" or "Here I am". Move the text widget from sidebar to sidebar. Look at your site after each move to see where the text shows up.

Again, the key thing to remember is that sidebars are containers for widgets and correspond to distinct areas of your website. Widgets are the building blocks that go into sidebars.

Adding Widgets

As we've discussed, if you go to *Appearance > Widgets* you'll see *Available Widgets* and the sidebar areas. The available widgets will vary according to the theme and the plugins that you're using. However, these widgets should always be present:

- Archives - This shows when you added blog posts.
- Audio - The audio widget allows you to embed an audio file into the sidebar. You add the audio file in the same manner that you'd add an image.
- Calendar - It would be lovely if this was a calendar of events. Nope. It's a calendar that shows when you made blog posts.
- Categories - This widget arranges your blog posts by category.
- Custom HTML - If you get raw HTML for a newsletter signup or for an affiliate like, use this widget to add it to the sidebar.
- Gallery - Use this to add a cute photo gallery to the sidebar.
- Image - This inserts images into your sidebars. The interface is just like adding images with the page or post editor.
- Meta - This used to be very popular, but is no longer used very often.
- Navigation Menu - This is the widget you'd use to add a custom menu.
- Pages - The pages widget is almost like another menu. It makes a list of your site's pages.
- Recent Comments - This makes a list of recent blog comments.

- Recent Posts - I've seen this used in websites with a blog page. You can add a list of recent blog posts to the sidebar in the pages.

- RSS - This displays blog posts from other blogs in your sidebar. If you have multiple websites you might use this to cross-promote your sites.

- Search - Use this to allow visitors to search your site for needed information.

- Tag Cloud - Like the meta widget, this one is no longer used very often.

- Text - Working with the text widget used to be complicated. No more. The text widget has a visual editor just like your page/post editor. There aren't as many icons, but there's enough to give you some great options when adding content to the text widget.

- Video - If you'd like to use this to add a YouTube video, click *Add Video.* Then select *Insert from URL* on the left to see a different interface.

To add a widget to a sidebar, click on the widget and drag it over to the sidebar. Pause for a moment, and the widget will be embedded in that sidebar. Then release and the widget is in place. You can drag the widgets around within a sidebar to reorder them.

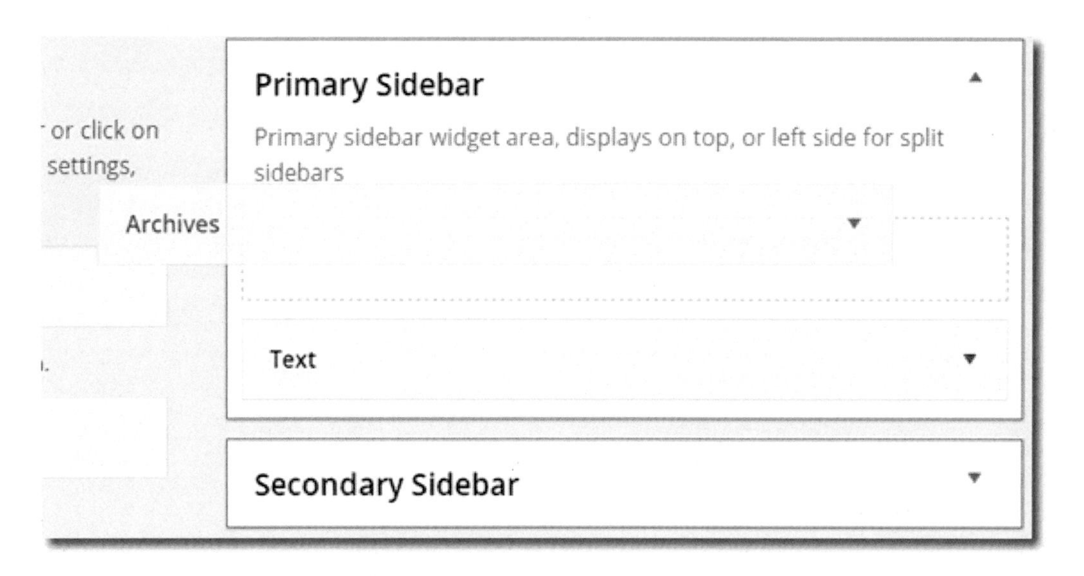

Let's go over that again. To add a widget to one of the sidebars you drag and drop it into place. Yes, it really is that easy.

If you'd like to delete a widget, drag it back to the inactive area. You can also expand it and click *delete*.

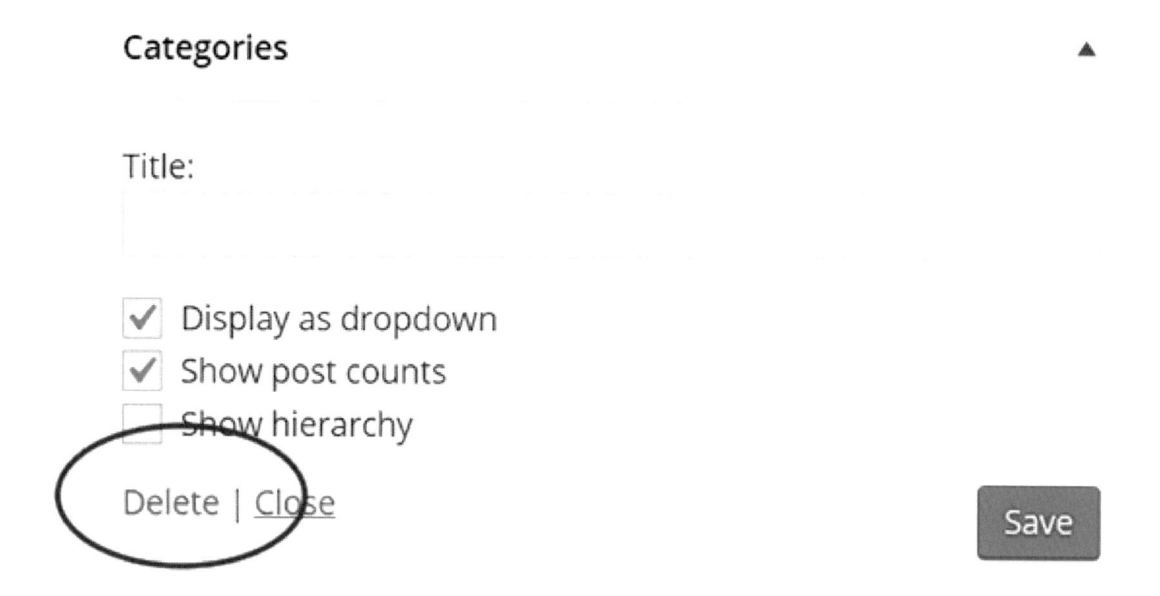

As you work with widgets, you deal with something that you can either think of as "an interesting feature" or "a crazy-making inconsistency". There is no *Save* as you add, move or delete widgets. If you drag a widget over to a sidebar then it's there. If you accidentally put a widget in the wrong spot, then it's there.

However, if you make a change inside the widget, like add a title to a category widget you *do* have to click on *Save*.

So, when you move widgets around you don't have to save. If you expand a widget and make a change to it (title, different features, etc.) then you *must* save those changes. What an interesting feature.

Search Engine Optimization

People have written entire books about Search Engine Optimization (SEO). It's a complicated subject and the rules of the game change frequently. I'll give you some basic concepts, but before I get into that, here are my two rules for SEO:

1. **SEO is a process.** What works today may be SEO poison next year. Things are in flux all the time. You'll need to continue to research and try new things to increase your SEO skills and knowledge. Persistence and thoughtful analysis are key.
2. **Content is king.** In the end, what really matters is your site's content. That's what it's all about. Be fascinated by your site's subject matter and readers will find your site (and you) fascinating. Search engine optimization is important, but without good content it doesn't matter.

The Basics of SEO

The process of getting your site to show up at the top spot in Google for a particular search term is called Search Engine optimization or SEO. Notice that I mentioned Google specifically. While there are other search engines like Yahoo and Bing, Google is by far the most popular search engine. My advice is to forget about the other search engines and focus on Google.

Site ranking is the order that websites appear on a search engine results page. This is extremely important. Studies have shown that most people will only look at the first page of results from a search engine. Also, people are more likely to click on links at the top of the list.

Google matches what people type in (we call these keywords or keyword phrases) with websites. So how does Google decide what sites are the best matches? That's the million-dollar question! The answer is that only Google knows. It has a search engine algorithm that gets updated periodically. While Google does share what it considers to be best practices it doesn't share exactly how it ranks sites. Also, things can change dramatically in Google's algorithm. Over time you'll see tried and true SEO practices fall out of Google's favor. (Remember, SEO is a process.)

Next, find a few keywords or keyword phrases that match your site. There are a few rules of thumb for picking keywords:

- A two or three keyword phrase is best. Imagine the difference between someone typing in "hotel" and someone typing in "Oregon hotel". Using two or three words will help you connect with your target market.
- Your keywords should be something that people will actually type into search engines. Scoring well for a phrase that no one uses won't help.
- Make sure that the keywords mirror your website content. If you're using "Oregon hotel" as your keywords make sure that your site uses that term instead of something like "Portland B&B".

The next step is to see how your site scores for those search terms. That sounds easy doesn't it? Just put your keyword phrase into Google and see where your site shows up. The problem is that our friend Google always tries to be helpful. It sees that you visit your site frequently. So if you put in a search term that's related to your site, it will give your site preferred treatment in the rankings that it shows you.

So how do you trick Google into showing you the rankings that *everyone* sees? Go to a browser that you rarely use. Make sure you're signed out of your Google account. Go to https://startpage.com. They anonymously submit searches to Google and then show you the results.

Enter your keywords into StartPage just as you would into Google, and make note of your results. Continue to log them over time as you work on SEO so you'll know what tactics are effective and which aren't.

In general good SEO tactics are to write about your keywords. Enter the keywords into titles of pages and posts. Answer questions that people have about the keywords. If you're not an expert on your chosen keywords, become an expert. Content really is king.

Recommended Plugin - All in One SEO Pack

There are also plugins that can help. All in One SEO Pack is my plugin of choice for SEO. It's flexible enough for the SEO novice as well as the SEO expert. This plugin has a lot of features and settings. If you're just getting started with SEO the default settings should be fine. To learn more about SEO, read the plugin's user guide.

Once the plugin is installed, click on *All in One SEO > Feature Manager* to activate the XML sitemaps feature. Sitemaps are lists of pages of your site. The plugin will make the sitemap and reach out to Google to let it know whenever your site is updated.

Google Analytics

Wouldn't it be nice to know how many people came to your website every month and what pages they looked at? Wonder no more! The answer to those questions can be found with a little help from a free service of Google. Google Analytics will collect all kinds of statistics on your website including:

- How long people stay on your site
- What are the most popular pages
- Who links to your site
- And much, much more

To get set up with Google Analytics, go to their site and set up your account. Then use All in One SEO Pack to add your Analytics ID to your site.

Go to *All in One SEO > General Settings* and then scroll down until you get to the *Google Settings section.* Enter your ID in the *Google Analytics ID* area.

To learn more about Analytics check out this free course:
https://analytics.google.com/analytics/academy/course/6

Social Media and Newsletters

While not exactly SEO, using social media and newsletters can also help bring traffic to your site. Remember when I said that Google changes its algorithm? Those changes can *dramatically* decrease your traffic overnight. Of course you can work on your SEO to get back into Google's good graces, but how are you going to get website traffic in the meantime?

You will need another plan to bring visitors to your site. Urge visitors to sign up for your newsletter. Send out a newsletter once a month so that people remember who you are. Have an active social media presence. Those things can save your bacon if you're on the losing end of a Google algorithm change.

Website Security

Website owners sometimes say, "I have a small site. Who would want to hack it?" The truth is that website hacks are rarely targeted at a specific site. A hacker will buy some hacking software. (Yes, *that* kind of software is for sale.) The hacking program will troll the Internet looking for sites that aren't maintained, have bad passwords or don't have security software.

If a site is hacked, a malware delivery system might be installed on the hacked site's server space. However, often a hack is a much more "simple" problem like injected code with links to pharmaceutical sites.

Just like there's no way to make your car 100% safe from car thieves, there's no way to keep your website 100% safe from hackers. However, much like with your car, we can make it difficult for the hacker to get into your site. The goal is to make your site so difficult to hack that the hacker (or the hacking program) will move along and leave you alone.

Your first line of defense is to have a good WordPress username and password.

Do not use "admin" as your username. For years that was the default username. The "bots" used by the hackers spend a lot of time and effort trying to guess WordPress usernames and passwords so that they can gain access to the WordPress dashboard. They *always* try admin as the username. Why make it easy for the hackers? Use something else.

Now let's talk about passwords. Do not use something easy and simple to remember. Those are all the qualities of a password that is easy for the bots to guess. It should be at least ten characters. It's best if it contains numbers, letters as well as special characters.

Backups and Updates

Now let's talk about updating your WordPress software, plugins and themes. Those all need to be updated periodically. You'll want to do those updates because having out-of-date software is frequently the reason that sites get hacked.

There are three steps to an update. First you back up your files. Then you update. Finally, you test.

Why the big production? I update WordPress sites on a regular basis. I've got sites of my own and I help my customers with their sites. About 98% of the time things go fine. You make updates just in case you get an unlucky roll of the dice and you have a problem. If you have an update you can roll back to your site's prior state OR you can give your backup to someone who can do that for you. Think of the backup as an insurance policy.

First things first, let's talk about the backup. Within your WordPress site there are two types of things to back up. The WordPress database contains the text of your pages and post. It also contains your site settings, comments and passwords. There are also website files. Your images, plugin files, theme files and WordPress files are all sitting on your website server. You'll want to back up both the database and the website files. There are a number of ways to do this:

- I use WP-DB-Backup to back up the database. Then I FTP a copy of the wp-content file folder, the wp-config file, and the .htaccess file to my computer.
- You could use WP-DB-Backup to back up the database. Then use File Manager, or another WordPress plugin, to back up the wp-content file folder, the wp-config file, and the .htaccess file.
- Your website host may have tools to help you backup your site. Call and ask them about it.
- I've also had good experiences with CodeGuard. It's a paid service that will back up your website files and databases.

I recommend that you keep the last three rounds of backups on hand. If something bad happens during an update, or if your site gets hacked, you'll want to have those files.

Once the backup is made, open the site in a fresh browser window. We'll call this Browser One. Remember to do this *before* the update. Open several tabs so you can see key pages like the home page, the blog, the contact page, or any mission-critical page. Browser One gives you something to compare your website to *after* the update. In other words, this is how you'll be able to test to make sure that your website looks the same after the update.

To actually update your WordPress software open a second browser window. The codename for this browser window is Browser Two. All of the updates are made in Browser Two. Go to *Dashboard > Updates*. The needed updates will be divided into three sections. At the top of the page you'll see if WordPress needs to be updated. Follow the instructions to update the WordPress software. In the plugin and theme sections you'll click beside each item that you want to update.

After the update, compare how your site in Browser Two looks with the view in Browser One. *Don't refresh the view in Browser One.* You're trying to compare how the site looked *before* the update with after the update. Do the sidebars still look the same? Is your navigation bar working?

If you have a contact form, fill it out and make sure you get the email. If you just updated an online shopping application, then make a test purchase. Make sure that your Google Analytics code is still working.

Problems After Update

As I said, there are rarely problems after WordPress updated. Odds are that everything will be fine when you update your site. Additionally, if there's a problem it will probably be a small one. I just want you to be prepared in case something happens.

So here we go, this is what you can do if there's a problem after the WordPress update.

- Take notes and/or screenshots of any error messages or problems that you see.
- If the problem is serious, put the site into maintenance mode. Then visitors to your website won't see your site looking less than its best.
- If the problem is with your contact form or shopping cart, contact the plugin maker and ask them for help. There's a *Support* button on the right side of every plugin page on WordPress.org.
- Try turning off your plugins to see if that takes care of the problem. To do that go to the plugins area and deactivate them all. If that fixed the issue, turn the plugins back on one at a time until you find the one causing the problem. Once you've identified the trouble maker, go to the plugin page at WordPress.org to see if other people are having the same trouble. Someone else may have found a fix for the issue or maybe you'll see an update from the plugin maker. If no fix is available, contact the plugin maker, or you may need to find another plugin.
- If the plugins aren't the problem, maybe it's the theme. Try switching to one of the default WordPress themes like Twenty Sixteen. To switch themes go to *Appearance > Themes* and activate a different theme. If the problem is gone, that indicates that your theme is the issue. Check with the WordPress forum or the theme developer for a possible fix.
- Contact your website host to see if they have any insight into the problem. Possibly a server issue developed at the same time you were doing the update. In other words, the issue may have nothing to do with the update. It doesn't happen a lot, but I *have* seen this happen.

WordPress Security Plugins

I use two security plugins, Sucuri Security and Cerber Security. Each one protects different parts of your site.

Sucuri scans for malware, hardens your site against hackers and can be a big help if you do get hacked.

You'll be asked to get a Sucuri API key. The plugin will walk you through the process. Next go to *Settings > Alerts.* I love Sucuri, but the default setting results in you getting many, many emails. Once you're familiar with the workings of your site, you might like to turn most of those alerts off.

On the *Hardening* tab you'll see that Sucuri wants you to get a website firewall. That's optional. Here are the most important settings for the hardening panel:

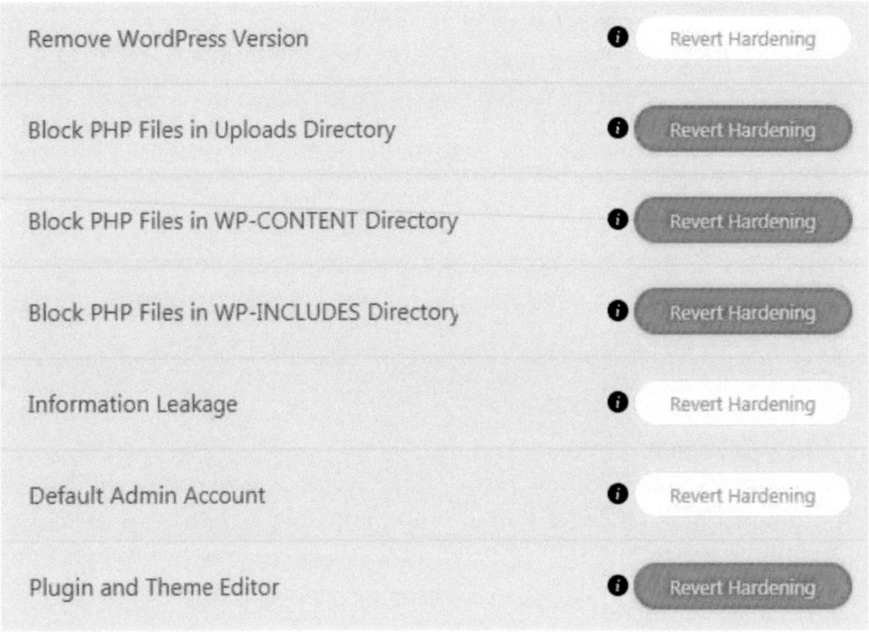

Remove WordPress Version — Revert Hardening

Block PHP Files in Uploads Directory — Revert Hardening

Block PHP Files in WP-CONTENT Directory — Revert Hardening

Block PHP Files in WP-INCLUDES Directory — Revert Hardening

Information Leakage — Revert Hardening

Default Admin Account — Revert Hardening

Plugin and Theme Editor — Revert Hardening

If you use any CAPTCHAs on your site, you'll want to check on them after hardening the wp-content folder. (CAPTCHAs are those are those funny letters that you have to type into a box before you submit a form.) If you have any problems with your CAPTCHA click *Revert hardening* for the wp-content area.

Remember when I talked about bots trying to guess the username and password combination for WordPress dashboards. That's called a brute force attack. Why such a harsh name? The bots don't just guess once and then go away. Nope. They can hammer away at your site, guessing and guessing again until your site slows to a crawl. To fight against that, I use the Cerber plugin. I also use Cerber to help stop comment spam.

Once you've installed Cerber go to *WP Cerber > Access Lists* and add your IP address to the *White IP Access List*. Then go to *Main Settings* and in the *Activity* section set the system to keep records for 7 days. That should give you enough data without bogging down your site's database. For additional information on configuring the plugin, go to the author's website at https://wpcerber.com/getting-started/.

One word of caution with Cerber, if you're using a PHP version less than 5.6.33 you may have problems. (If you don't know what version of PHP you're using, your website host should be able to tell you.) A better choice for you might be the Loginizer plugin.

Troubleshooting

I've been helping customers with WordPress for years. These are some of the common problems that pop up.

Toolbar Icons are Different

The visual view of the editor and the text view of the editor have different icons. Make sure that you're looking at the editor in the *visual* view.

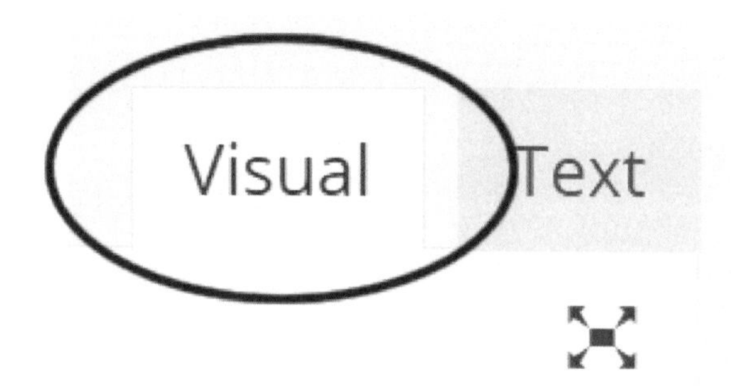

Toolbar is Missing the Bottom Row

What if the second row of icons suddenly disappears? What if the second row of icons has never been there? That's because of the Toolbar Toggle. Click the button and you'll see the second row of controls.

Missing Post or Page

As we've discussed, the whole page and post thing can take some getting used to. I've had numerous clients say things like, "I made a new post, but I don't see it in the system. I *swear* that I saved it." And so they did. They saved it as a page instead of a post. So if you're missing a post, take a quick look through the pages to see if it's there. If you're missing a page, look at the posts. Once you've found the missing document just copy and paste it to the proper location.

WordPress 5

WordPress 5 is scheduled to be released sometime in 2018. The reason that I'm addressing it here is that it will include a major change. WordPress 5 will redo the editing area. Instead of having something that's as familiar to you as your email screen, you'll have a new editor called Gutenberg. It's not user friendly and I am not a fan.

Currently Gutenberg is a plugin. As of this moment, it only has a tree-star rating out of a possible five stars. 171 out of 369 reviews give it just one star.

In addition to the difficulty in using the new editor, themes and plugins may break when WordPress 5 is installed. In other words, WordPress 5 may break thousands of WordPress sites.

Folks, fasten your seatbelts. It's going to be a bumpy night.

At this point, here's my advice.

- **Contact your website host and make sure that the auto update function on your site is turned off.** You do not want to be updated to WordPress 5 automatically. You probably won't want to make the move to WordPress 5 for a few months. Let them work the kinks out before you make the change.

- Check to see if other people using your theme and plugins are having problems with WordPress 5. If they are, wait until those bugs are fixed before the update.

- Ask your host or website developer if they can help you make a staging area or development environment wherein a test version of your site can be updated to WordPress 5. If it works there, then you can update the live version of the site.

Mostly, we just have to wait and see what happens. There's talk about keeping Gutenberg a plugin. There are also people who are building a plugin based on the current WordPress editor. We just don't know how this situation is going to end. Watch my blog at www.perryweb.com for updates on this situation.

Resources

Here's a list of helpful websites.

- https://www.perryweb.com/ - This is my website. Check out my blog for helpful articles about working with WordPress.
- https://wordpress.org/ - This is where you'll get free WordPress plugins and themes. If you ever have a problem be sure to check out the forum.
- http://www.brokenlinkcheck.com/ - This site helps you identify broken links.
- https://moz.com/ - Interested in learning more about SEO? This website has loads of information!
- http://www.problogger.net/ - This site has a wealth of knowledge for people wanting to make money blogging online.
- https://www.siteground.com/go/pic - SiteGround hosts my website. I highly recommend them. They offer amazing technical support and tools to manage your website.

Before you go, I want to thank you for buying my book. I hope you've found it helpful. I know there are a lot of books about working with WordPress on the market. The fact that you selected my book means a lot. Thanks!

If you have a second, would you mind leaving a review on Amazon.com? I'd love to hear what worked for you and what didn't. Was the book too technical or just about right? Would you like to see more information on another topic?

To get more information about WordPress, sign up for my newsletter at www.perryweb.com. You might also enjoy my Facebook page.